SOMETHING TO OFFER

A Guide to Giving

BISHOP SHERMAN ALLEN

SCGA Ministries

Copyright © 2025 by SCGA Ministries

All rights reserved. No part of this book may be reproduced, stored in a retrieval system, or transmitted in any form or by any means—electronic, mechanical, photocopying, recording, or otherwise—without the prior written permission of the publisher, except in the case of brief quotations used in articles or reviews.

All Scriptures are taken from the King James Version (KJV) of the Holy Bible, which is public domain in the United States, unless otherwise indicated.

Scripture quotations marked (NKJV) are taken from The New King James Version®. Copyright © 1982 by Thomas Nelson. Used by permission. All rights reserved.

Greek and Hebrew word references are taken from *Strong's Exhaustive Concordance of the Bible* by James Strong, S.T.D., LL.D., which is in the public domain.

ISBN: 979-8-9994908-0-3

Printed by Kingdom Publishing & Printing, Houston, TX in the United States of America

First Edition

PASTORS SERIES

Something To Offer

TWELVE OFFERTORY OUTLINES FOR GIVING

DEDICATION

Something To Offer *is dedicated to the legacy and memory of my late grandfather, Supt. Solon Gee and and father, Supt. Sherman Gee, who were my greatest preaching influences. To my stepfather, Bishop Edward Allen, who was my greatest prophetic influence and to my late mother, Clarice Warren Allen, who taught me the importance of rigorous academic study and true spirituality.*

I also owe a tremendous debt of gratitude to my spiritual fathers and mentors who now watch from the portals of Heaven: Dr. Albert E. Chew, Bishop G.E. Patterson, Bishop A. LaDell Thomas, Sr. and Bishop J.L. Johnson, all of whom have left indelible spiritual imprints upon my life and ministry; and, to my Presiding Prelate, Bishop R.J. Burt, who has been a tremendous source of strength, support, intercession and inspiration.

*Special thanks to my beloved wife, Dr. Otonya Eskridge-Allen, and to our children who have given your support in this labor of love, to Dr. Gloria and Rev. James Word for your academic support; and, to our amazing Executive Team: Executive Pastor Laura O'Neal and Minister Pamela Anderson, for your invaluable and unwavering commitment and unyielding sacrifice of your gifts, time and talents in order to bring **Something To Offer** to fruition, in both word and deed.*

To Grace International Fellowship, Prophetic Ministries Covenant Alliance, Inc. (PMCA) and Christ Cathedral Church family for your continuing covenant commitment both in Ministry and in life.

Finally, please allow me to offer my most sincere appreciation to two of my dearest friends, Dr. Dana Carson and Bishop Liston Page II for your contributions of faith, friendship and fellowship reflected in and beyond the pages of this book.

CONTENTS

Foreword	ix
Prologue	1
Preface	5
1. Outline # 1 *Firstfruits*	17
2. Outline # 2 *Tithes - Part 1: How to Sanctify Your Money*	22
3. Outline # 3 *Tithes - Part 2: How to Open The Windows of Heaven*	27
4. Outline # 4 *Tithes - Part 3: The Blessing of Melchizedek*	33
5. Outline # 5 *Power To Get Wealth*	36
6. Outline # 6 *Good Success Vs. Bad Success*	40
7. Outline # 7 *Planted Like A Tree*	43
8. Outline # 8 *Good Measure, Pressed Down, Shaken Together And Running Over*	48
9. Outline # 9 *Let Down Your Nets*	53
10. Outline # 10 *Seedtime And Harvest*	60
11. Outline # 11 *No Man Can Serve Two Masters*	64
12. Outline # 12 *Money In The Mouth Of The Fish*	77
Epilogue	81

FOREWORD

It can be difficult to find a single book that covers all aspects of tithes and offerings. However, this work seeks to provide a complete look at the issue from a biblical standpoint.

A book for the present and times to come...***Something To Offer: A Guide To Giving***, presents a practical and theological framework for pastors to teach tithing and offerings in a way that speaks to 21st-century Christians, particularly those influenced by economic insecurity, digital giving, and concerns about institutional trust.

Bishop Sherman Allen has penned a work for leaders of congregations, a well-designed book that will be a vital tool for pastors navigating the tension between biblical tradition and modern skepticism around giving. Each chapter provides knowledge and actionable steps that operate as a catalyst to guarantee that a ministry functions with excellence in a fiduciary capacity.

Bishop Sherman Allen, through serious research and years of experience, presents 12 outlines that are thorough and concise which will not only excite but inspire readers from all walks of life, whether in the Church House or the Market Place. It is my conviction that this work should be obligatory reading for not only pastors but laity as well. This will ensure that everyone is on

FOREWORD

the same page when it comes to establishing financial stability in the House of God and in the lives of the reader. *"...Bring the whole tithe into the storehouse, so that there may be food in my house, and thus put me to the test, says the Lord of hosts; see if I will not open the windows of heaven for you and pour down for you an overflowing blessing"* (Malachi 3:10, NRSV).

--Bishop Liston Page II, D. Min., S.T.M., author of *How to Survive Your Storm & Battle Strategies for Spiritual Success!*

PROLOGUE
What's in Your Heart?

*J*oshua 7:21-25 details the story of a young man named Achan who, after Israel's victory at Jericho, takes of the spoils from the city a *"goodly Babylonian garment, and two hundred shekels of silver, and a wedge of gold of fifty shekels weight,"* and when no one was looking, hid and buried them in his tent rather than sacrificing them unto the Lord. Although Joshua had commanded that all of the spoils (silver, gold, vessels of brass and iron) were to be consecrated unto the Lord and brought into the treasury of the Temple (Joshua 6:19), Achan, because of covetousness and greed, decided to violate the commandment and steal the goods for himself. Although the exact value of the stolen offering is not mentioned, we do know that two hundred shekels of silver and 50 shekels of gold would have been significant, given that one shekel weighed approximately eight to twelve grams. The monetary values then, at minimum, would have been about 1600 grams of silver and 400 grams of gold (or, $1728 for the silver and $108,200 for the gold, at today's prices, respectively). Needless to say, whatever the monetary value was, the moral components of disobedience and disregard were far more weighty than the value in money. Firstly, because as the spoil of Jericho, the first city in Canaan, this would have been a type and shadow of the tithe of the Promised Land. Secondly, Achan's disobedience brought a curse upon Israel as a whole and caused them to be defeated at Ai. Thirdly, the gravity of Achan's disobedience was so significant that he was stoned to death because of his sin.

The story of Achan reminds us that our tithe and offerings represent our covenant with God, our commitment to honor Him in all things and our continuing dependence upon Him for future success. No amount of money warrants disobedience to the Word of God nor departure from the principles and practices of worship as a means of daily devotion. Matthew 16:26 says, *"For what is a man profited, if he gain the whole world, and lose his soul?"*

The test of giving causes us to choose between trust and temptation; between duty and desire; and between obedience and opportunity. The issue for Achan as well as for us is not just what can I hold on to when no one is looking, but rather what can I offer when only God is looking. Whether in the accounting of Heaven or on earth, if an audit is all that keeps us from stealing, then the issue is not with what's in our hands but with what's in our hearts.

What we withhold or release from our hands reveals what's in our hearts. Our priorities, our passions, our goals, our desires, our habits and our proclivities can all be determined by a quick glance at our checkbook, bank account, credit card statement or financial "tents."

Matthew 6:21 and Luke 12:34 both say, *"For where your treasure is, there will your heart be also."* Often we think that individual gifts or purchases are an anomaly, but when we look at patterns over time, they reveal whether we are selfish or charitable, pragmatic or ostentatious, misanthropic or philanthropic. Our treasures are a reflection of our values, our virtues and our vices. They reflect what drives and motivates us internally.

Oftentimes, what we are busy doing with our hands makes us overlook, or ignore, what's happening in our hearts.

Several years ago, I was traveling and preaching a rigorous schedule of an average of two or three cities per week, typically six to nine months each year. In fact, I became so driven that I later realized that I had worked almost 5 five years without taking a real vacation that was not work or ministry related! I was easily preaching thirty outside engagements per year in addition to at least forty Sundays in our home church. And, because I was young and relatively healthy, or so I thought, I was able to fulfill the assignments of my hands without affecting my heart. I was a Pastor, a husband and a father fulfilling each role with "all" of my heart! I remember vividly in what I thought was a routine physical exam, the doctor saying that something looked "slightly abnormal" with my EKG and she wanted to refer me for additional testing. After performing a stress test and a nuclear stress test, they determined that they needed to perform a cardiac catheterization in order to determine what was going on. When the cardiologist finished the initial procedure, he found that I had three out of four arteries all blocked more than ninety percent. They performed an emergency procedure where they inserted two stints. The doctor was amazed that with my schedule of travel, stress and physical exertion I had experienced no symptoms of pain or discomfort.

Furthermore, he told me that with the amount of blockage that I had it would have "most certainly eventually resulted in a heart attack" and that I would have only had **six minutes** to get medical attention before it would have most likely been fatal. The startling revelation for me, both physically and spiritually, was that all of that time I had no idea what was happening in my heart!

I hope and pray that as you read the pages of this book, it

will not only encourage you to examine what's in your hands but also to examine what's in your heart. Jeremiah 17:9 says, *"The heart is deceitful above all things, and desperately wicked: who can know it?"* Hopefully, the time spent reading and reflecting upon matters of giving and receiving will remind us that what is often hidden in the recesses of our hearts is not revealed until the most critical times. And, what is most precious also has the potential to be most poisonous.

As we examine the following pages, we will do ourselves well to examine our own moral, spiritual and fiscal "tents" and to excavate those things that we have hidden and kept from consecrating them as sacrifices to the Lord. We must also remember the admonition of Luke 12:48.

> *"For unto whomsoever much is given, of him shall much be required: and to whom men have committed much, of him they will ask the more."*

While we are balancing budgets, we must also be cognizant of balancing all of the gifts that God has given us.

PREFACE

The concept of offerings began in the Bible narrative when Adam would meet God in the *"cool of the day."* Specifically, Adam would meet to worship and offer unto God the *"yadah,"* which means "the extension of the hands" (Hebrew). This daily time of worship most probably involved the giving of the "tithes" from the *"tree of knowledge of good and evil."* (Genesis 2:9) This tree and the fruit thereof were a biblical type and shadow of the tithe since it belonged to God and man was forbidden from eating or consuming it.

The second reference to an offering in the Bible takes place when Adam sinned in the Garden of Eden. Genesis 3:21 says, *"Unto Adam also an*d *to his wife did the Lord God make coats of skins, and clothed them."* Here, the offering is a foreshadowing of sacrifice and redemption which would take place through Jesus Christ, the lamb of God slain before the foundation of the world. *"Without the shedding of blood, is no remission..."* (Hebrews 9:22). The next specific reference to offerings takes place in Genesis 4 with the narrative of Cain and Abel. The scripture says in Genesis 4:3-4 that *"Cain brought of the fruit of the ground an offering unto the Lord. And Abel, he also brought of the firstlings of the flock* (tithes) *and the fat thereof* (offering)."

Although it is not the purpose of this text to be exhaustive in our discussion of the topic of giving, as we study we find that the concept of offerings is deeply rooted and embedded in Hebrew culture and worship. The Book of Leviticus, for example, details five types of offerings that were required in Jewish worship. They were the burnt offering, grain offering, peace offering, sin offering and guilt offering. Each of these offerings represent and foreshadow the life, ministry and sacrificial death of Jesus Christ for the sins of mankind. Of course, we should also note that the concept of offerings is not unique to Jewish and Christian worship. In fact, there is in almost every worship tradition some form or conceptualization of offerings, whether practical or philosophical, as a requirement for, or as part of, worship. Our offerings connect our heads, hands and hearts to God.

The purpose of this discourse is to provide context and content for Christian Ministers who want to approach the practice of offertory worship with scriptural integrity. Because of the various misuses and abuses of the "giving moment" during religious worship services, many people are offended by the idea of giving and receiving offerings. It is often associated with fraud, greed and manipulation from the pulpit and results in distrust and disdain from the pew. For this reason, my advice to Ministers who honestly want to finance the legitimate work of the Kingdom of God, while understanding the various nuances of balancing budgets along with maintaining a lifestyle that is conducive to Bible principles is simply this: **PROCEED WITH CAUTION.**

THREE INTERNAL MOTIVATIONS

Every offertory appeal should have three internal motivations:

1. LOVE FOR GOD

Deuteronomy 6:5 establishes the primary motivation for the relationship between mankind and God. *"And thou shalt love the Lord thy God with all thine heart, and with all thy soul and with all thy might."*

In verses 10-12, Moses connects love for God to the idea of thanksgiving, reverence, commitment and devotion.

> *^{10} "So it shall be, when the LORD your God brings you into the land of which He swore to your fathers, to Abraham, Isaac, and Jacob, to give you large and beautiful cities which you did not build, ^{11} houses full of all good things, which you did not fill, hewn-out wells which you did not dig, vineyards and olive trees which you did not plant —when you have eaten and are full — ^{12} then beware, lest you forget the LORD who brought you out of the land of Egypt, from the house of bondage. (NKJV)*

It is important to understand that love for God requires, at its core, appreciation for the blessings and benefits afforded to us by virtue of our relationship with Him. Appreciation then, becomes the basis for giving.

Without a proper context of appreciation for that which has been given, the requirement (or request) to give can easily be misinterpreted as being contrived or born out of manipulation. Simply stated, **giving is an act of love.**

The challenge for every Minister who embarks upon the task of receiving an offering in the name of the Lord is to ensure that his appeal is because of his love for God and not because of his love for money. Too often we value the gift above the giver. Paul writes in 1 Timothy 6:10-11, *"For the love of money is the root of all evil: which while some coveted after, they have erred from the faith, and pierced themselves through many sorrows. But thou, O man of God, flee these things; and follow after righteousness, godliness, faith, patience (and) meekness."* When an appeal to give is motivated by love for God rather than love for money, it exudes and embodies the attributes of God and results in meekness of Spirit rather than arrogance of the flesh. God is a giver by nature. John 3:16 reminds us, *"For God so loved the world that He gave His only begotten son…"* When we focus on our love for God and His love for us, it releases the SPIRIT OF GIVING, rebukes the SPIRIT OF GREED and repels the SPIRIT OF OFFENSE.

2. LOVE FOR GOD'S PEOPLE

In the parable of the Good Samaritan Jesus reminds us that the greatest commandments require our Love for God and our love for each other. This point is plainly elucidated in Luke 10:27.

> *"And he answering said, Thou shalt love the Lord thy God with all thy heart, and with all thy soul, and with all thy strength, and with all thy mind; and thy neighbor as thyself."*

In verses 29-37, the response of the lawyer in the text, as well as the ensuing parable of the unnamed neighbor who was wounded on his way from Jerusalem to Jericho, describes and demonstrates the callous indifference of horizontal religion without vertical relationship. The lawyer represents a religious system couched in legalism and exclusivity. Jerusalem represents the place of worship and sacrifices offered to God. Jericho represents the place of service and sacrifice to humanity outside of the walls of the Temple. The victim in the text, is wounded on the journey between "worship" inside the walls and the place where worship should produce the work of community outside of the walls. When he was attacked by thieves, those who were religious (the priest and the Levite) overlooked his wounds and ignored his need for assistance. The Samaritan approached him, rendered aid and paid for his care. His offering was a representation of love shared vertically to mankind while the priest and the Levite were only interested in expressing love to God within the walls of the Temple. In other words, our love must be both vertical and horizontal.

In 1 John 3:17 we are admonished, *"But whoever has this world's goods, and sees his brother in need, and shuts up his heart from him, how does the love of God abide in him?" (NKJV)*

Whenever we receive offerings, we must not only be cognizant of our love for God, but we must also be sensitive to the needs of God's people. While we must challenge their faith in giving, we must also ensure that our offertory appeal does not demean their inability to give what is requested. If you have ever sat in a Worship Service and felt embarrassed or berated because you were unable to give what was asked (or, sometimes demanded), then you know that the feeling you experienced in that moment certainly didn't feel like it was motivated by love. Love always seeks to lift, encourage and inspire even when we are not able to meet desired expectations. **GOD NEVER REQUIRES WHAT WE ARE UNABLE TO GIVE.** 1 John 5:3 says, *"For this is the love of God, that we keep his commandments: and, his commandments are not grievous."* If we leave the offering feeling grieved rather than edified, then the request was probably not motivated by love. Sometimes what we call building faith is simply, bullying through fear.

3. TRUST IN GOD'S PROVISION

Too often men and women of God challenge our parishioners to "walk by faith and not by sight" (2 Corinthians 5:7) when in fact, our offertory appeals are motivated by fear rather than by faith. 'What if we don't meet the budget?' 'We're not leaving until we get what we need.' 'If we don't get it, it won't be done.' Statements like these are more of a reflection of our own fear that a particular need might not be met, rather than a reflection our faith in God's provision.

As a Pastor for more than 40 years, I have had many times that a particular need (or financial goal) was not met during the offering, but afterwards God would touch the heart of someone to release a seed, even if they weren't in the Service or didn't hear the appeal. I've learned to trust God's people to hear His voice and to allow His voice to speak louder than mine. My voice should always be an echo of what He has said or what He is saying in the earth realm. When He speaks Heaven and earth respond.

The ability to trust in God's provision is deeply rooted in three prevailing principles: Firstly, God has whatever I need. Psalm 24 says, *"The earth is the Lord's and the fullness thereof; the world, and they that dwell therein."* Secondly, not only is God able to provide, but He **will** provide. Philippians 4:19 says, *"But my God shall supply all your need according to his riches in glory by Christ Jesus."* Thirdly, God is not limited to the resources that are visible and available to me. In Esther 4:14, Mordecai reminded Esther of something that we often forget: God can do whatever He desires through whomever He desires. He is not dependent upon our obedience. *"For if you remain completely silent at this time, relief and deliverance will arise for the Jews from another place..."* A God who can use serpents, rocks, rods, donkeys, roosters, lions, bears and fish to meet the needs of his people, is certainly not limited to 10 minutes of an offertory appeal in any given room on any given Sunday! Hebrews 11:6 says, *"Without faith it is impossible to please him: for he that cometh to God must believe that He is, and that He is a rewarder of them that diligently seek him."* OUR FAITH MUST BE IN THE PROVIDER AND NOT IN THE PROVISION. Whether He rains down manna from Heaven, uses a little meal in a barrel or multiplies bread and fish from a sack lunch prepared by a mother for her son, it's still God's sovereign provision from His unlimited supply! While we are awaiting the provision, we have to also trust the process.

Additionally, in our faith walk as Ministers, there are times when we, as a matter of faith, have to say to the people, 'that's enough!' In Exodus 36:5-7 after the people of God had obeyed in giving, the offering was more than enough.

> *5 And they spake unto Moses, saying, The people bring much more than enough for the service of the work, which the Lord commanded to make.*
> *6 And Moses gave commandment, and they caused it to be proclaimed throughout the camp, saying, Let neither man nor woman make any more work for the offering of the sanctuary. So the people were restrained from bringing.*
> *7 For the stuff they had was sufficient for all the work to make it, and too much.*

Because we serve a God of more than enough, there should be times when those of us who trust God for provision should be able to say, "We have more than enough!"

When was the last time you heard a preacher say, "Don't give anymore; we have more than enough?"

ONE METHODOLOGY

"Thy word have I hid my heart that I might not sin against thee." (Psalm 119:11)

While there are thre primary internal motivations for an Offertory Appeal, there should only be one methodology. That is that every appeal must be rooted in the principles of the Word of God. Every other methodology is rooted in witchcraft and results in manipulation! In 1 Samuel 15:23 we are told that *"Rebellion is as the sin of witchcraft, and stubbornness is as iniquity and idolatry."* What is interesting is that the context of the scripture in this text is that Saul has chosen to keep (as an offering) what God had told him to discard. He kept the best of the possessions of Agag, the King of the Amalekites, and that which was *"vile and refuse they utterly destroyed."* (v. 9) The text makes abundantly clear that Saul's issue was iniquity (hidden, unconfessed sin) and idolatry. In other words, an offering that is derived merely for self gain in the name of a *"sacrifice unto the Lord,"* (v. 15) rather than in obedience to the Word of the Lord, is the result of sin. This type of sin is witchcraft (a willful attempt to manipulate the will or actions of another). Scripture provides for us the proper context for determining what God requires versus what we desire; it discerns and delineates the *"thoughts and intents of the heart."* (Hebrews 10:12) It is also important to note that when the prophet Samuel pointed out Saul's sin, he still tried to manipulate the Word of the Lord in order to justify his actions. Proper application of scripture in the offertory appeal then, should include content (what it says), context (why it says what it says and what it means) and conviction (allowing the Holy Spirit to do the work through the Word without emotional manipulation or excuses). When the appeal is based upon need or greed, rather than trust and obedience, it lends itself to overt (or covert) manipulation because it is motivated by desire rather than by faith. When Jesus tells us in Matthew 6:24 *"no man can serve two masters... you cannot serve God and mammon (money),"* He is literally reminding us that when dealing with matters of finance we must choose between obedience to God and obedience to money (whether it is the need for it or the lack of it).

ONE MANTRA

Where God guides, He provides.

As a final note, it is important to remember that GOD GIVEN PROVISION IS THE RESULT OF GOD GIVEN VISION. Simply put, check your vision before raising an offering because the 'objects in the mirror are closer than they appear.' In other words, once you focus on provision through the "windshield," it's easy to become distracted from vision in the rear-view mirror. Vision must always be the focal point of every appeal and when vision is God ordained and God inspired, provision will eventually catch up with you! Provision always obeys the speed limit.

THREE LITMUS TESTS OF VISION

1. Is it God - Inspired?

The two primary elements that determine the answer to this question are introspective. Namely, can it be definitively traced to a moment where "God breathed" this particular vision into the earth realm for His glory? And, can it be traced to a particular scripture for the purposes of doctrine and practice? Genesis 2:7 says, *"And God breathed into man the breath (ruach) of life and he became a living soul (nephesh)."* It is the Spirit of God that inspires the mind, will, desires and emotions of man. And, without God inspired vision, people perish (become overwhelmed or cast off restraints.) Proverbs 29:18

> *Where there is no revelation, the people cast off restraint;*
> *But happy is he who keeps the law.*

2. Is it competition driven?

In order to answer this question with honesty and integrity, it requires both introspective reflection and external observation. Is the vision motivated by a "keep up with the Jones" mentality? What is your "measure of Grace" in a given area of ministry? Do you have the capacity (bandwidth, patience, skill sets, etc.) for this particular endeavor? Luke 14:28, 31 says, *"For which of you, intending to build a tower, does not sit down first and count the cost, whether he has enough to finish it—*

(Verse 31) Or what king, going to make war against another king, does not sit down first and consider whether he is able with ten thousand to meet him who comes against him with twenty thousand?"

Could it be that what we often call "faith" is actually our excuse for poor planning and competition dressed up in church clothes? Furthermore, embedded in the idea of whether a particular vision is competition driven is the question of time and season. The question is not just, 'Am I called to do it?' The question is, 'Am I called to do it now?' Ecclesiastes 3:1-11

> *1 To every thing there is a season, and a time to every purpose under the heaven:*
> *2 A time to be born, and a time to die; a time to plant, and a time to pluck up that which is planted;*
> *3 A time to kill, and a time to heal; a time to break down, and a time to build up;*
> *4 A time to weep, and a time to laugh; a time to mourn, and a time to dance;*
> *5 A time to cast away stones, and a time to gather stones together; a time to embrace, and a time to refrain from embracing;*
> *6 A time to get, and a time to lose; a time to keep, and a time to cast away;*
> *7 A time to rend, and a time to sew; a time to keep silence, and a time to speak;*

> *8 A time to love, and a time to hate; a time of war, and a time of peace.*
> *9 What profit hath he that worketh in that wherein he laboureth?*
> *10 I have seen the travail, which God hath given to the sons of men to be exercised in it.*
> *11 He hath made every thing beautiful in his time: also he hath set the world in their heart, so that no man can find out the work that God maketh from the beginning to the end.*

3. Is it based upon "need vs. greed," "devotion vs. emotion," or "mission vs. permission?"

What particular need does the vision meet within your specific community demographic? Is it birthed out of a life of devotion or a moment of emotion? Is it motivated by "mission or permission? Simply put, just because you have the means to do a thing doesn't mean that you are 'called' to do it.

Now, that we have explored the origins and motivations for Giving and Receiving, we are ready to delve into the Biblical principles and teachings of ***"Something to Offer."***

Remember that your offering is not just an issue of what's in your hand, it's also an issue of what's in your heart. 2 Corinthians 9:7 says, *"Every man according as he hath purposed in his heart, so let him give; not grudgingly, or of necessity; for God loveth a cheerful giver."*

Something To Offer

OUTLINE # 1

Firstfruits

The history of Firstfruit offerings is deeply rooted in Hebraic worship. Firstfruits were a voluntary offering which represented the best of something given in gratitude for harvest as a token of acknowledgment of provision. The Hebrew word, "*Re'shiyth*," signified that which was first in place, time, order and rank. In Bible history, Adam was a "type and shadow" of the "Firstfruit" of mankind. Abraham was "Firstfruit" of the faithful. Joseph was "Firstfruit" of the Children of Israel in Egypt. Jericho was "Firstfruit" of the promise in Canaan. Ruth and Naomi were the "Firstfruit" who returned back to Bethlehem Judah at the beginning of Barley Harvest, and Jesus Christ was the "Firstfruit" of them that slept. The term Firstfruit is also rendered *"bikkuwr"* with regard to crops.

The earliest mention of Firstfruits in the Bible was related to offerings given as a result of Harvest and commemorated in the House of the Lord. Times and manner of these special offerings were outlined in Exodus 23:16 and 19; Leviticus 23:10,17 and 20; Numbers 18:20 and Deuteronomy 26:10. In the New Testament, the theme of firstfruits primarily refers to the Holy Spirit and the resurrection of believers in Romans 8:23; I Corinthians 15:20 and 23; James 1:18 and Revelation 14:4.

As you study you will find that the firstfruit offering is both celebratory and reciprocative. Although it is categorized as one of the "Freewill" offerings, it is clear that it is given in thanksgiving for, in response to, and in respect of the Harvest (or increase) that has been given by God. Simply stated, firstfruits are given out of a grateful heart!

Exodus 23:16,19 says, *"And the feast of harvest, the firstfruits of thy labors, which thou hast sown in the field...The first of the firstfruits of thy land thou shalt bring into the house of the Lord thy God..."*

Leviticus 23:10-11,17 and 20 describe the process of bringing the firstfruits to the priest and the priest offering it as a "wave offering" unto the Lord. Here, it is a "type" of resurrection (sheaf of the wave offering v.15) and a "type" of Pentecost (loaves of the wave offering v.17,20). The **Firstfruits** offering then, is **personal, corporate and progressive.**

The primary focus of **firstfruits** is **honor** rather than **obedience**. Proverbs 3:9-10 says, *"Honor the Lord with thy substance and with the Firstfruits of all thine increase: So, shall thy barns be filled with plenty and thy presses shall burst out with new wine."*

THREE TESTS OF HONOR
1. PRIORITY

> *"But seek ye FIRST the Kingdom of God, and his righteousness; and, all these things shall be added unto you."* Matthew 6:33

Just as the farmer must plant the seed before the harvest, the believer sows the seed as a matter of priority in honor of the One who has provided the seed, knowing that the ground, the seed and the harvest all belong to the Lord. If he consumes the seed before he plants it, then it yields no harvest because he has prioritized appetite above honor.

God gives us **substance** to honor Him. Whatever we place before God (either as a matter of priority or proximity) becomes an idol. Exodus 20:3 says, *"Thou shalt have no other gods before me."*

2. PORTION

In Proverbs 3:9 the word substance, *"hown"* (Hebrew) means "wealth, riches, sufficiency, best, enough." It literally means all that you can carry, or give, at one time! It reminds us that everything that we possess has been given to us to honor God. The word "honor," in the text is *"kabod."* In the Hebrew it means to "glorify, promote, or to make abundant or glorious in appearance and weight."

Numbers 18:12 says, *"All of the best of the oil, and all of the best of the wine, and of the wheat, the firstfruits of them which they shall offer unto the Lord, them have I given thee."* God's portion must always be our best part! In this sense it doesn't mean quantity or amount, as it does with the tithe. It means quality or the best part. As it has often been said, 'we give God what is right and not what is left.' Whenever God gives increase, we owe him the best portion.

3. VALUE

"Matthew 6:21 says, *"Where your treasure is, there will your heart be also."*

Our treasure, *"thesauros"* (Greek) means "a deposit of that which is valuable; repository, storehouse."

When we give offerings of sacrificial value, we store up treasures in Heaven. Matthew 6:19-21 says, *"Lay not up for yourselves treasures upon earth, where moth and rust doth corrupt, and thieves break through and steal: But lay up for yourselves treasures in Heaven, where neither moth nor rust doth corrupt, and where thieves do not break through nor steal: For where your treasure, is there will your heart be also."* Honor and treasure are two sides of the same coin! When we honor God with our substance, it reveals His place in our lives, and He releases a greater portion to us. Proverbs 3:10 says,*"So shall your barns be filled with plenty and your presses shall burst out with new wine."* Barns sygnify that which is laid up for the future; storehouses (In a contemporary context, it refers to savings accounts, 401k's, stocks, bonds, annuities, investments, etc.).

The word presses, *"yeqeb"* (Hebrew), means "to excavate; a trough that is dug out; wine vat, or a wine press; whether the lower one into which juice drains; or the upper one where grapes are crushed."

*I*n other words, the promise for honoring God with the firstfruits of our increase is that God will bless our savings to be full and that we will never run out because our presses (whether wine presses or money presses) will always be replenished.

That's exactly what happened with the widow at Zarephath of Zidon in 1 Kings 17! Because she gave the Prophet Elijah the firstfruits of the cake that she was going to make for herself and her son, *"her meal barrel wasted not."* In other words, it never ran out and she became a repository for a drought-stricken community until God caused it to rain again. She had *"more than enough"* because she honored God with her first portion! (1 Kings 17:9-16)

Something To Offer

OUTLINE # 2

Tithes - Part 1: How to Sanctify Your Money

Leviticus 27:30-31

> *30 And all the tithe of the land, whether of the seed of the land, or of the fruit of the tree, is the Lord's: it is holy unto the Lord.*
> *31 And if a man will at all redeem ought of his tithes, he shall add thereto the fifth part thereof.*

The primary difference between **firstfruits** and **tithes** is that firstfruit offerings are voluntary and do not require a set amount. Tithes, on the other hand, are mandatory and are designated as the "first tenth." In fact, the word tithe literally means "tenth." It is important to note that the children of Israel paid three types of tithe and each tithe was designated for a different purpose. The first tithe was the **Levitical Tithe** which was dedicated to the care of the Levites who were responsible for Temple Service. This was especially significant because the Levites were not apportioned land as an inheritance in

Canaan. The tithe then, was their inheritance as a part of the priesthood. The second tithe was the **Festival Tithe** which was used to support the 7 Annual Religious Festivals in Israel. The first two tithes were paid annually. The third tithe was the **Poor Tithe** which was paid every three years and was set aside for the care of the poor, including widows and orphans. Failure to tithe was considered robbing God (which we will discuss more thoroughly in a subsequent outline). Suffice it to say, the context of Levitical offerings was established both for honor and support with the understanding that the tithe belonged to God. Any violation of the Law of the Tithe was considered a violation of the Mosaic Law. It is for this reason that some Christian ministers mistakenly teach that tithing is under the law and is therefore no longer required under the New Covenant. As we discuss the origin of the tithe with regard to the law, two things should be noted on the subject of tithing:

Firstly, prior to the Mosaic Law there existed types and shadows of the tithe including the fruit of the *tree of knowledge of good and evil* in the Garden of Eden, Abel's offering, Abraham's offering of the "tithe" unto Melchizedek, and his offering of Isaac, as well as Joseph's entrance into Egypt. All of these types predated and preceded the codification of the Tithe into the Law of Moses; and, secondly, the requirement of tithing as a practice continued in the New Testament and was endorsed by Jesus in Matthew 23:23 and by Paul in Hebrews 7:4-9. The subject of tithing, in regards to the law, will be discussed more thoroughly in Outlines 3-4.

For the sake of our present outline, I want to consider the text in Leviticus 27:30. *"...All the tithe of the land, whether of the seed of the land, or of the fruit of the tree, is the Lord's..."*

All of the tithes belong to the Lord. (referring to all three types of tithes and all tithes derived from every **increase**)"...

Because this scripture is written in the context of an agrarian culture, there are two categories:

1. The Seed of the Land refers to that which is sown for future increase and consumption. In our contemporary context, it would refer to social security, taxes, insurance, tax deferred annuities, investments, etc. Therefore, it means we tithe from our gross income rather than from our net income.

2. The Fruit of the Tree refers to that which is available for consumption. (i.e. net income)

It is important to note that we pay tithes on both seed and fruit, not either/or. For instance, if you pay tithe from the gross income you pay on both seed and fruit; but if you get a tax refund, an insurance settlement, dividends from investments, or income from mortgages, loans, inheritances, etc. then you pay tithe **again** because now it is an **increase** due to interest earned or unexpected income **(harvest)**. The spiritual principle is explained in 1 Corinthians 3:6 in the context of a harvest of soul winning, *"I have planted, Apollos watered; God gave the increase."* Since God controls the time and amount of the harvest/increase and there are times when conditions yield no appreciable increase, whenever God gives increase, then we owe tithe. The type of harvest does not change the scriptural principle.

Often people ask, 'Why should I pay tithe on money when I have already paid tithe on it?' Or, 'Why should I pay tithe on a loan when it is technically not an increase?' The answer is easily understood if you have ever lost money on stocks or other investments or if you have ever been denied for a loan for which you applied. Whether it is through allowing the economy or the market to perform well or allowing you to meet the lending criteria of a particular financial institution, it is God who gives the "increase!" The only questions that determine whether or not you should tithe on a particular amount of money is, "Is it more than you had before and/or does it give you access to more than you had?" If the answer is, 'yes,' then you should pay tithe based upon the biblical principle of Leviticus 27:30. Generally speaking, if it is "taxable" then it is also "tithable." However, taxes can be deferred legally, but tithes cannot be deferred. What is first, by definition can **never not** be first, by position or priority.

The tithe is holy (sanctified) unto the Lord *"... it is holy unto the Lord."*

The Hebrew word for holy is *"qodesh"* which means "a sacred place or thing; consecrated; set apart; sanctified." It signifies that the tithe is set apart for God's exclusive use. The tithe, 1st tenth cannot be used for secular purposes and once sanctified, the part that is sanctified, sanctifies the whole. The part of the land given to the Levites was sanctified as their inheritance. It also sanctified the inheritance of all the tribes of Israel because of their obedience, as the priest bore their sins. Numbers 18:21-23

> **21** *And, behold, I have given the children of Levi all the tenth in Israel for an inheritance, for their service which they serve, even the service of the tabernacle of the congregation.*
>
> **22** *Neither must the children of Israel henceforth come nigh the tabernacle of the congregation, lest they bear sin, and die.*
>
> **23** *But the Levites shall do the service of the tabernacle of the congregation, and they shall bear their iniquity: it shall be a statute for ever throughout your generations, that among the children of Israel they have no inheritance.*

The Penalty for Disobedience (with regard to the tithe)

"And if a man will at all redeem aught of his tithes, he shall add thereto a fifth part thereof." (Leviticus 27:31)

The word redeem in the Hebrew is *"ga'al."* It carries the context of a "kinsman redeemer" or one who buys back (or redeems) property as the next of kin. The idea is that the kinsman redeemer acts as a purchaser to prevent loss. In this case, redeeming the tithe has to do with holding back (or buying back) that which belongs to God for the purpose of preventing loss or to pursue personal gain.

The penalty for redeeming (holding back) the tithe is 1/5th or 20%.

Specifically, *"he shall ADD thereto the FIFTH PART thereof."* In other words, 20% (interest) + 10% (original tithe) = 30%. When you hold back what belongs to God, He considers it a loan for which He charges 20% interest. Because the tithe is an obligatory statute, it cannot be altered nor amended without violating the principle of ownership, and therefore robbing God. (Malachi 3:8)

Something To Offer

OUTLINE # 3

Tithes - Part 2: How to Open The Windows of Heaven

Malachi 3:8-12

> 8 Will a man rob God? Yet ye have robbed me. But ye say, Wherein have we robbed thee? In tithes and offerings.
> 9 Ye are cursed with a curse: for ye have robbed me, even this whole nation.
> 10 Bring ye all the tithes into the storehouse, that there may be meat in mine house, and prove me now herewith, saith the Lord of hosts, if I will not open you the windows of heaven, and pour you out a blessing, that there shall not be room enough to receive it.
> 11 And I will rebuke the devourer for your sakes, and he shall not destroy the fruits of your ground; neither shall your vine cast her fruit before the time in the field, saith the Lord of hosts.
> 12 And all nations shall call you blessed: for ye shall be a delightsome land, saith the Lord of hosts.

The concept of an "Open Heaven" does not originate with the tithe. Actually, the first time Heaven was opened was in the context of Judgment. In Genesis 7:11-12, we read, *"In the six hundredth year of Noah's life, in the second month, the seventeenth day of the month, the same day were all the fountains of the great deep broken up, and the windows of Heaven were opened. And the rain was upon the earth forty days and forty nights."* When the windows of Heaven were opened, the earth could not contain what was poured out! The **outpouring** resulted in **overflow**! At the beginning of the Old Testament, in the Book of Genesis, and at the end of the Old Testament, in the Book of Malachi, God uses the windows of an "Open Heaven" to send a flood of overflow, of judgment in Genesis and of blessing in Malachi.

In Malachi 3:8 God tells the children of Israel that their departure from His ordinances and subsequent disobedience in tithes and offerings has robbed him of the opportunity to bless them and has instead caused the entire nation to be cursed. Just as the disobedience of mankind caused the earth to be cursed and the disobedience of Achan caused the entire nation to forfeit the victory at Ai, so the disobedience of Israel in the text, has caused the entire nation to be cursed again. When God admonishes them to repent and return unto Him, they ask, *"Wherein shall we return?"* God responds with a question, *"Will a man rob God?"* They then respond, *"Wherein have we robbed thee?"* And, God answers, *"In tithes and offerings."* It is interesting to note that every place in the text where God references judgment or repentance, He ties it to an offering.

In verse 3, He says that he shall *"sit as a refiner and purifier of silver: and purify the sons of LEVI* (the recipient of the TITHES) and *"purge them as gold and silver, that they may offer unto the Lord an offering in righteousness."* In verse 4 He says, *"Then shall the offering of Judah and Jerusalem be pleasant unto the Lord, as in the days of old, and as in former years."* And, again in verse 8, He says, that in order to break the curse that has come upon them, they must return *"in tithes and offerings."*

In Malachi 3:8-12, God gives the Promise of Blessings for Obedience in Two Parts:

PART 1. The 2-Fold Requirement: BRING and PROVE

"BRING ye all the tithes (all 3 types as well as that which is delinquent) *into the storehouse, and PROVE me now herewith, saith the Lord of hosts..."*

The word storehouse, *"owtsar"* (Hebrew) means "depository, armory (as in cache of weapons); treasury; supply or store of food and drinks."

The word prove, *"bachan"* (Hebrew) means "to test, or put to trial; investigate, examine or scrutinize." It should be noted that this is the only place in Scripture where God invites man to "test" (Bachan) him legitimately without it being portrayed as being sinful and arrogant. God, then, considers the tithe as an appropriate place for the *"trying of our faith."* (James 1:3-4)

PART 2. The 5-Fold Results

Result: *"I will open YOU the Windows of Heaven..."* which implies a two-dimensional opening:

1. for you (FROM ABOVE)
2. within you (FROM WITHIN).

It is significant to note that when God got ready to end the drought during the days of the prophet Elijah in 1 Kings 18:42-45, Elijah went up to the top of Mt. Carmel, fell upon the earth, put his face between his knees and said to his servant, *"go up and look toward the sea... and at the seventh time, he said there ariseth a little cloud out of the sea, like a man's hand...and... the Heaven was black with clouds and wind...there was a great rain."* Here, prophetically, there is both a looking up and a looking within before Heaven is opened.

Result: *"I will pour you out A BLESSING..."* infers a continuous stream of blessing."*It maketh rich and adds no sorrow with it.*" (Proverbs 10:22). The word rich "*bashar*" (Hebrew) means "to grow rich, to enrich, or to become rich or wealthy." The connotation has to do with material possessions. The word sorrow, "*esseb*" (Hebrew) means "pain, hurt, toil, labor, hardship, or offense." In this passage, the BLESSING promised, is that the tithe releases an easy FLOW. While Proverbs 10:22 refers to individual blessings, Genesis 12:2-3 refers to a flow of generational blessings:

7-fold Blessing of Abraham (Genesis 12:2-3)
"I will make of thee a great nation.
I will bless (Barak) thee.
I will make your name great. (Reputation)
I will make thee a blessing. (Missions)
I will bless them that bless thee. (Reciprocity)
I will curse them that curse thee; (Defense)
and, in thee shall all families of the earth be blessed." (Witness)

"*I will pour you out A BLESSING...that there shall not be room enough to receive*" refers to the blessing of overflow on three levels of manifestation:

1) Extent which has to do with capacity. It specifically denotes depth in terms of, 'how much can you hold or contain?'

2) Enlargement deals with width or, 'how much can you manage?' It determines your level of stewardship. Simply put, it specifies how much you can maintain without waste.

3) Expansion signifies, 'how much can you carry for the purpose of sharing or dispersing to others?' This level represents missions and outreach.

When your blessing becomes someone else's miracle, you have reached overflow! The promise of overflow is that blessings exceed capacity so that your biggest challenge becomes, "Who can I bless next?" When you are living in the realm of Malachi

3:11 and Luke 6:38, you must always remember that what God puts in your hands is not just for you.

> *Give, and it shall be given unto you; good measure, pressed down, and shaken together, and running over, shall men give into your bosom. For with the same measure that ye mete withal it shall be measured to you again.* Luke 6:38

Result: *"And, I will rebuke the devourer.."* simply means that God will always protect His investment. The word rebuke literally means, "STOP! That's enough!" Here the tither is reminded that God will always protect His investment and defend what belongs to Him. Devour, *"akal"* means "to eat, to burn up, to consume." The promise here is that the seed will not be eaten up before it is planted, nor will the harvest be destroyed before it is produced. Malachi 3:11 *"... and He shall not destroy the fruit..."*

> *No weapon that is formed against thee shall prosper; and every tongue that shall rise against thee in judgment thou shalt condemn. This is the heritage of the servants of the LORD, and their righteousness is of me, saith the LORD.* Isaiah 54:17

Result: *"Neither shall your vine cast her fruit in the field before time."* God controls the season of increase although there are times when it looks like the harvest is delayed. What looks like a delay is actually a promise against premature delivery.

> *Verily, verily, I say unto you, Except a corn of wheat fall into the ground and die, it abideth alone: but if it die, it bringeth forth much fruit.* John 12:24

Result: *"And all nations shall call you blessed: for ye shall be a delightsome land, saith the Lord of hosts."*

Just as Genesis 12:3 promises blessings **for** every generation, Isaiah 60:3-6 promises blessings **from** every nation.

> *3 And the Gentiles shall come to thy light, and kings to the brightness of thy rising.*
> *4 Lift up thine eyes round about, and see: all they gather themselves together, they come to thee: thy sons shall come from far, and thy daughters shall be nursed at thy side.*
> *5 Then thou shalt see, and flow together, and thine heart shall fear, and be enlarged; because the abundance of the sea shall be converted unto thee, the forces of the Gentiles shall come unto thee.*
> *6 The multitude of camels shall cover thee, the dromedaries of Midian and Ephah; all they from Sheba shall come: they shall bring gold and incense; and they shall shew forth the praises of the Lord.*

The promise is that enemies of every ethnicity, especially Gentiles, will participate in, decree and declare blessings over you.

Something To Offer

OUTLINE # 4

Tithes - Part 3: The Blessing of Melchizedek

enesis 14:18-20

> *18 And Melchizedek king of Salem brought forth bread and wine: and he was the priest of the most high God.*
> *19 And he blessed him, and said, Blessed be Abram of the most high God, possessor of heaven and earth:*
> *20 And blessed be the most high God, which hath delivered thine enemies into thy hand. And he gave him tithes of all.*

Melchizedek is a type of Jesus Christ, as both King and Priest. The text tells us that he is the King of "Salem" (peace; a prototype of Jerusalem). As the "Priest of the Most High God" (*El Elyon*, Hebrew) he presents the enduring and everlasting Priesthood of Jesus Christ, as opposed to the Aaronic Priesthood, which was often ended by death. Also, as a type of Christ, he brings forth *"bread and wine"* and gives it unto Abram. Of course, bread and wine foreshadows the Eucharist in the New Testament and reminds us that the tithe bridges the gap between Old and New Testament, in both practice and principle, prophetically and dispensationally. Genesis 14:18-20, when read in conjunction with Hebrews 7:1-10, clearly shows the continuation of the tithe—transitioning from the Old Testament to the New—through the priestly office of Jesus Christ. It moves from the Aaronic priesthood to the priesthood of Christ, which is after the order of Melchizedek.

In both texts, Melchizedek typifies *Jesus Christ as both King and Priest*. In Genesis 14:17, he is "King of Salem" and "priest of the most high God" and in Hebrews 7:2-3 he *"King of righteousness and ... King of Salem, which is King of Peace; without father, without mother, without descent, having neither beginning of days, nor end of life, but made like unto the son of God; abideth a priest continually."*

In both texts, the tithe is connected to and is the result of victories over enemies who have been defeated and had their spoils taken away. In the Old Testament it refers to the slaughter of the King of Chedorlaomer and the kings who were confederate with him, as well as the rescue of Lot, his goods and the people who were taken captive with him. In the New Testament it refers to spiritual victories over sin, death, Hell and the grave. It represents both rescue and resurrection.

In both texts, the Greater (Melchizedek) blesses the lesser (Abram) and the lesser pays tithes as a result of the blessing.

In Hebrews, the Priesthood of Melchizedek is greater than the Priesthood of Aaron because:

- Abram paid tithe to him before it was required by the Law (v. 4).
- Levi, who received tithe of his brothers, also paid tithe while he was yet in Abram's loins which signifies that tithing secures a GENERATIONAL BLESSING (v. 5-6, 9-10); and
- Tithing is perpetual by virtue of the perpetuity of the everlasting priesthood of Jesus Christ (v. 8).

Further evidence that tithing does not end with the Old Testament Law, is that Jesus affirmed the tithe in both principle and practice in Matthew 23:23, as he rebuked the Pharisees for tithing while ignoring the *"weightier matters of the law, judgment, mercy and faith..."* In specifically addressing the practice of tithing in the New Testament, He says, *"these ought ye to have done, and not to leave the other undone."* In other words, the New Covenant does not exempt the believer from tithing. It expands the requirement to tithe while also practicing justice, mercy and faith.

Something To Offer

OUTLINE # 5

Power To Get Wealth

euteronomy 8:18

> *But thou shalt remember the Lord thy God: for it is he that giveth thee power to get wealth, that he may establish his covenant which he sware unto thy fathers, as it is this day.*

The key component in giving to God is remembering that everything that we have, came from Him. My dear friend, Bishop Richard "Mr. Clean" White often said, "What we know, He taught us; Where we are, He brought us; What we have, He gave us; and What we are, He made us."

Giving then, becomes an act of remembrance and reciprocity.

There is a phrase that ministers often quote when receiving offerings. 'It is not as a debt you owe but as a seed you sow.' Although it sounds good, technically when you give, it is both DEBT and SEED. It is a debt of **gratitude** and **thanksgiving**, but it is also a seed of **faith**!

Deuteronomy 8:18 begins with the words, *"But thou shalt remember the Lord thy God…"*

The word remember, *"Zakar"* (Hebrew) means "to mark, to recall or to call to remembrance; to make a memorial."

In this context, remember literally means "to choose not to forget." It is an active verb. In Deuteronomy 8:2-10 Moses admonishes Israel to remember and to rehearse in their minds all of the ways that God had sustained them through 40 years in the wilderness between Egypt and Canaan.

In verses 2-6 He reminds them of God's sustenance through suffering in order to humble them and to prove them.

HOW HE SUSTAINED THEM (V. 2-6)

1. Manna "What is it?" (v. 3)

Can you imagine being lost in the wilderness without food or water for 40 years? And during that time, every day, six days a week, for 40 years, God rained down bread from Heaven. Six days x 52 weeks x 40 years = 12,480 times God sent bread to feed them! Without a grocery store, supermarket, a garden or farm, job or paycheck, God fed them **everyday**. However, He only allowed them to take what they could consume that day except on Friday, when He gave them enough to last through the Sabbath (Saturday). As the bread came down from Heaven, they called it, "Manna" because the word Manna literally means, ***"What is it?"***

2. Clothes *"Raiment waxed not old; neither did thy foot swell, these 40 years."* (v. 4) Can you imagine wearing the same clothes and shoes for 40 years without them becoming torn or tattered; and, without gaining or losing weight so that you wear the same size today that you wore 40 years ago? Or can you imagine walking around for 40 years in the same shoes without getting holes in the soles of your shoes or without even a pedicure?

HE SECURED LAND FOR THEM THAT DID NOT BELONG TO THEM (V. 7-9)

1. *"He gave them land with fountains and springs, hills and valleys* (v.7)
2. *He gave them wheat and barley, vines, fig trees, pomegranates, olive oil and honey* (v. 8)
3. *He allowed them to eat all that they wanted; there was no scarcity and no lack"* (v.9)

HE SAID UNTO THEM, *"WHEN THOU HAST EATEN AND ARE FULL, THEN THOU SHALL BLESS THE LORD THY GOD FOR THE GOOD LAND WHICH HE HATH GIVEN THEE." (DEUTERONOMY 8:10)*

The word, bless, "*barak*" (Hebrew) means to "kneel, bow, praise, salute; bestow, as an act of adoration."

In verses 11-20 He said unto them to "Beware that you forget not the Lord..." Here, he warns them against pride, arrogance and self-confidence as a result of the blessing of the Lord. In verse 17, he says, *"And thou say in thine heart, My power and the might of mine hand hath gotten me this wealth."*

HE REMINDED THEM THAT GOD WAS THEIR SOURCE.

> "But thou shalt remember the Lord thy God: for it is He that giveth thee the power to get wealth, that he may establish his covenant which he sware unto thy fathers, as it is this day." (V.18)

The word power, *"koach"* (Hebrew) means, "capacity, means, ability, strength, might." God reminded the children of Israel that their intellectual and physical dexterity came from Him. Every idea, every plan, every invention and every gift came from Him.

Wealth, *"chayil"* (Hebrew) refers to all resources, whether human, fiscal, intellectual, tangible or abstract. It includes that which is gained by force or earned by labor. James 1:17 reminds us that *"Every good gift and every perfect gift is from above, and cometh down from the Father of lights, with whom is no variableness or shadow of turning."*

Moses reminds us that not only does the POWER to get wealth come from God, but also that the PURPOSE of wealth is to reflect God's covenant promises in the earth and to advance the Kingdom, generationally and dispensationally.

Something To Offer
OUTLINE # 6
Good Success Vs. Bad Success

Joshua 1:8

This book of the law shall not depart out of thy mouth; but thou shalt meditate therein day and night, that thou mayest observe to do according to all that is written therein: for then thou shalt make thy way prosperous, and then thou shalt have good success.

In Joshua 1:8, the idea of "good success" is a concept that proceeds out of focusing and meditating upon the Word of God. After the death of Moses, God encourages Joshua to *"be strong and very courageous"* in order to prosper *"whithersoever"* he would go. The idea here is that true prosperity is based more upon internal motivation than external factors.

The spiritual and intellectual challenge of course, is that if "good success" exists, then "bad success" must also exist. Generally speaking, we would assume intuitively that success by definition, is good. However, for the purpose of this discussion and in the context of Joshua 1:1-9, let's define "good success" as that which draws us closer to God, keeps us focused on His plan and purpose for our lives and fulfills destiny. "Bad success" then, means that which distracts us from God, and from accomplishing His purposes and plan for our lives. Success is not about what we attain or accomplish. It is about what we leave in the earth as a monument to God's purpose and plan for our lives and what we leave as a blessing to others. It includes worth, work and witness. "Bad success" includes that which engenders misplaced priorities, pride, arrogance and wasted potential. In our previous discourse we reflected upon the fate of Achan in the context of Mark 8:32. *"For what shall it profit a man, if he shall gain the whole world and lose his own soul?"* Achan was the victim of "bad success." because of MISPLACED PRIORITIES.

Secondly, in Luke 12:13-21 in the context of covetousness over an undivided inheritance, Jesus warns, *"Take heed and beware of covetousness, for one's life does not consist in the abundance of the things he possesses." (v. 15)* (NKJV)

He further relates a parable of a rich man whose ground produced plentiful crops. After surveying his barns and realizing that he did not have room to store all of his harvest, he decided to build bigger barns. In verse 19 he said, *"I will say to my soul, Soul thou hast much goods laid up for many years; take thine ease, eat, drink and be merry."* He is successful, but his success is "bad success" because of his PRIDE AND ARROGANCE.

The third instance of "Bad Success" for the purpose of our discussion was caused by WASTED POTENTIAL. In Matthew 25:15-28, Jesus tells a parable of servants who are given five talents, two talents and one talent, respectively. The two servants who were given five and two multiplied their talents, while the servant who was given one talent buried it. Upon close examination of the parable, four things are clear:

1. That the servant who buried his talent felt that it was insignificant or insufficient.

2. That he was motivated by fear more than by greed.

3. That he was envious of his masters' ability to reap a harvest from the labor of others.

4. That he never felt that his success was ever actually his, so he wasted his potential rather than enriching someone else.

v. 24 says, *"Then he which had received the one talent came and said, Lord, I knew thee that thou art a hard man, reaping where thou hast not sown, and gathering where thou hast not strowed. And, I was afraid and went and hid thy talent in the earth: lo, there thou hast that is thine."*

We will discuss this parable in further detail in a later outline with respect to proper motives for gaining and using wealth from a Kingdom perspective. In Joshua 1:8 we are reminded that "good success" requires three things: courage, focus on the promises of God and willingness to make it happen. In the context of this scripture, *"make thy way prosperous"* (make, *"tsalach"* (Hebrew), means "to push forward, break out, advance." It means that good success requires us to partner and participate with God.

Something To Offer

OUTLINE # 7

Planted Like A Tree

salm 1:1-3

> *1 Blessed is the man that walketh not in the counsel of the ungodly, nor standeth in the way of sinners, nor sitteth in the seat of the scornful.*
> *2 But his delight is in the law of the Lord; and in his law doth he meditate day and night.*
> *3 And he shall be like a tree planted by the rivers of water, that bringeth forth his fruit in his season; his leaf also shall not wither; and whatsoever he doeth shall prosper.*

There is nothing more powerful than a **time** and **purpose** whose **season** has come! In Ecclesiastes 3:1 Solomon says, *"To everything there is a season, a time to every purpose under the heaven."* Seasons are determined by calendar dates and weather, but time and purpose are determined by God. Growing up in North Central Texas, I became familiar with the fact that generally the most violent storms occur during the change between one season and another. It's not unusual to see multiple tornadoes within weeks, or even in one night between spring and summer. Whenever one season is trying to hold on and refuses to let go while another season is trying to emerge, the most violent storms occur. While storms can be disruptive and destructive, sometimes storms also carry seed from one field or region to another, so that crops that were previously not indigenous to one place begin to sprout in that place. Oftentimes it's the storms of life that remind us that one season is over and another season is beginning. It's often the storms that bring us to the place that will help us grow, become fruitful and multiply.

In Psalm 1, the Psalmist describes the elements and process by which we come to be planted by God and by which our lives yield fruitful productivity. Being planted and yielding a fruitful harvest requires three things: the right soil, the right seed, and the right season. The text in Psalm 1:1-3 details the practical process of each requirement. The word, blessed, *"esher"* (Hebrew) means "happy and fruitful." In order to receive and maintain the blessing of the Lord, the psalmist gives these prerequisites:

The right soil requires actions of righteous. (Psalm 1:1)

1. *"Not walking in the counsel of the ungodly"* requires walking in Godly WISDOM. It means that our progress (walking or moving forward) is not measured merely by profit, but by the ability to make wise and righteous decisions.

Proverbs 16:16 says, *"How much better it is to get wisdom than gold! and to get understanding rather to be chosen than silver!"*

2. *"Not standing in the way of sinners"* requires that our WITNESS must be such that it represents God in every area of our lives and does not hinder those who don't know Him from seeing Him in us.

In Acts 1:8, Luke says *"And you shall receive power ("dunamis") after that the Holy Ghost is come upon you, and you shall be* **witnesses** *"martus" (Greek) unto me both in Jerusalem "peace" (Greek) and in Judaea "praise" (Greek) and in Samaria (guardianship) and unto the uttermost part of the earth."*

3. *"Not sitting in the seat of the scornful"* requires that we are not quick to judge others or to make a mockery of the WAYS of God or His people. It means not joining in association with others who cause division, derision or disdain through gossip or slander.

Proverbs 6:16-19

> **16** These six things doth the Lord hate:
> yea, seven are an abomination
> unto him:
> **17** A proud look, a lying tongue, and hands
> that shed innocent blood,
> **18** An heart that deviseth wicked imagina-
> tions, feet that be swift in running to
> mischief,
> **19** A false witness that speaketh lies, and
> he that soweth discord among brethren.

Jesus teaches us in the Parable of the Sower that there are 4 types of Soil (Matthew 13:18-23)

- By the wayside (those who receive the Word without understanding)
- Stony ground (those who receive the Word with Joy and are subsequently offended by tribulations and persecution)
- Among thorns (those who receive the Word and allow the cares of this world and the pursuit of riches to make the Word unfruitful)
- Good ground (those who receive the Word by hearing and understanding; they produce fruit one hundredfold, sixty-fold and thirty-fold)

The right seed is the Word of God. (Psalm 1:2)

1. To take pleasure in the Law (statutes, ordinances, commandments) of the Lord means that His commandments are not onerous or burdensome; and

2. That he continuously meditates (concentrates upon, speaks or utters) the Word of God.

- Psalm 119:105 *"Thy word is a lamp unto my feet and a light unto my path."*
- Psalm 119:11 *"Thy word have I hid in my heart..."*
- Psalm 119:97 *"O how love I thy law! It is my meditation all the day."*
- Psalm 119:165 *"Great peace have they which love thy law: and nothing shall offend them."*

The right season denotes an atmosphere of faith. (Psalm 1:3)

1. *"Tree planted by the Rivers of Water"* (Genesis 2:11-14) 4 Rivers in the Garden of Eden:

- Pison - "increase" from within (Hebrew) which means Praise
- Gihon - "bursting forth" from beneath (Hebrew) which means Prayer
- Hiddekel - "rapid flow" from above (Hebrew) which means Prophecy
- Euphrates - "fruitfulness" (Hebrew) which means Productivity

2. *"He shall bring forth his fruit in his season..."* (Genesis 8:22) In the realm of the Spirit, there are only two seasons: "seedtime and harvest"

3. *"His leaf shall not wither…"*

4. *"Whatsoever he doeth shall prosper."* The word prosper, *"tsalach"* (Hebrew), means *"to push forward, advance, break out, succeed, be profitable."* In other words, when the right seed is planted in the right soil, in the right season, God will bless "whatever" you do!

Something To Offer

OUTLINE # 8

Good Measure, Pressed Down, Shaken Together And Running Over

Luke 6:38

> *Give, and it shall be given unto you; good measure, pressed down, and shaken together, and running over, shall men give into your bosom. For with the same measure that ye mete withal it shall be measured to you again.*

It is important to note that the text in Luke 6:38, although often taught as a scripture on giving, is actually taught by Jesus in the context of love, forgiveness and being forgiven as a part of his teaching on The Beatitudes. He focuses not just on the ACT of giving but also upon the proper ATTITUDE for giving.

Literally, where there is no "forgiving," it hinders whatever we are "giving for." This verse in Luke 6 then, must be understood in the full context of verses 20-38 (also, Matthew 5:3-12, 20-24). Jesus reminds us that giving of gifts to God must also include reconciliation and forgiveness. Matthew 5:23-24 says, *"If you bring your gift to the altar and there remembereth that thy brother hath ought against thee; leave there thy gift before the altar, and go thy way; first be reconciled to thy brother, and then come and offer thy gift."* The context of forgiveness is also consistent throughout Luke 6:20-38. Too often we fail to connect the unfruitfulness of our seed to our unwillingness to forgive. We cannot have faith to give and not have faith to forgive. Galatians 5:6 reminds us that *"... faith worketh by love."* For the purpose of our current discourse, let's then look at the progression from Luke 6, verses 27-38:

v. 27 Love your enemies

v. 28 Bless them that curse you

v. 29-30 Do not retaliate

v. 31 Do unto others as ye would have them do unto you

v. 32-34 The law of love extends beyond those who love us

v. 35 Do not give (or lend) for gain

v. 36 Be merciful

v. 37 Do not judge but forgive

v. 38 Give, and it shall be given

The challenge when we look at the proper context of giving, is that what we give with our hands can only be "blessed" when it is given with a right heart. Unfortunately, most of our teaching on giving focuses on the action of giving and receiving rather than on the attitudes that determine whether or not the seed is acceptable. Subsequently, we fail to understand the lesson of Cain, and then we are disappointed when we get the results of Cain's offering. In order for the principle of giving and receiving to work, the practice must be congruent with scripture.

When v. 38 says, *"Give and it shall be given unto you,"* it refers to both MANNER AND MOTIVE.

"Good measure, pressed down, shaken together and running over" refers to METHOD AND AMOUNT.

When I was a boy growing up in my parents' house, one of

my chores during the fall was to rake the leaves in the yard. As I would fill each bag with leaves, in order to get more leaves in the bag, I would shake the bag, press it down and then continue to add more leaves until the bag would overflow. Then, I didn't understand that I was learning a major theological principle about giving and the practice of receiving.

Namely, that when we give offerings, God uses shaking and pressure to give us more! When God allows circumstances to shake us and to press us down, He is only making room for more. It is also important to note that God uses men to bless us. Giving and receiving is relational. *"Shall men give into your bosom"* doesn't necessarily mean that the same men that you blessed, will come back and bless you. However, it does mean that because you have blessed others, the way that you blessed them now becomes a seed for your harvest. Showing mercy, forgiving and giving to others activates the LAW OF RECIPROCITY and the LAW OF ATTRACTION.

When we connect giving and forgiving three things happen:

1. We receive not only from what we sow, but we also receive a harvest from how we sow.

2. We activate and secure provision for future vision. *"...Into your bosom..."* means that there are dreams, visions, goals and desires in your heart that you have not yet realized; but when you give, your seed activates and procures provision in the hearts of those who have been predestined to sow into you.

3. Giving breaks cycles. Breaking a cycle begins with a seed. (Genesis 26:12-13)

> **12** Then Isaac sowed in that land, and received in the same year an hundredfold: and the Lord blessed him.
> **13** And the man waxed great, and went

forward, and grew until he became very great:

Isaac's seed broke the cycle of repeated famine.

The connection between Luke 6:38 and Genesis 26:12-23 is that Isaac trusted God enough to not fight for blessings that caused his enemies to envy him. **He chose to forgive rather than to fight.**

He attracted the envy of the Philistines (Genesis 26:14-16)

A. They stopped up the wells that his father had dug
B. They excommunicated him and sent him away
C. He pitched his tent in valley of "Gerar," "a (temporary) lodging place" and dwelt there

He digs again the wells of his father (Genesis 26:17-19)

A. He called them by the same names that his father had called them
B. While digging in the valley they found a well of "springing water"

He attracts the envy of the "herdsmen" of Gerar who said, "the water is ours." (Genesis 26:20-22) Three of four wells:
A. "Esek," (Hebrew) "Contention"
B. "Sitnah," (Hebrew) "Strife"
C. "Rehoboth," (Hebrew) "The Lord hath made room for us" and "we shall be fruitful in the land"

And every time he moved, God blessed him with more!

He went from digging holes and sowing seed to digging wells in the valley. The only difference between a hole and a well is that a well is a hole where you just keep digging until you hit water.

The Fourth Well was "Beersheba," (Hebrew) "well of a Sevenfold Promise" (The Covenant Promise of Abraham); It is also the Agreement (Covenant) made between Abraham and the Philistine King, Abimelech. (Genesis 12:2-3)

1) I will make of thee a great nation.
2) I will bless you.
3) I will make your name great.
4) I will make you a blessing.
5) I will bless them that bless thee.
6) I will curse them that curse thee.
7) In thee shall all the families of the earth be blessed.

There he digged a well, built an altar and pitched his tent.

Something To Offer

OUTLINE # 9

Let Down Your Nets

uke 5:1-11

> *1 And it came to pass, that, as the people pressed upon him to hear the word of God, he stood by the lake of Gennesaret,*
> *2 And saw two ships standing by the lake: but the fishermen were gone out of them, and were washing their nets.*
> *3 And he entered into one of the ships, which was Simon's, and prayed him that he would thrust out a little from the land. And he sat down, and taught the people out of the ship.*
> *4 Now when he had left speaking, he said unto Simon, Launch out into the deep, and let down your nets for a draught.*
> *5 And Simon answering said unto him, Master, we have toiled all the night, and have taken nothing: nevertheless at thy word I will let down the net.*
> *6 And when they had this done, they inclosed a great multitude of fishes: and their net brake.*

7 And they beckoned unto their partners, which were in the other ship, that they should come and help them. And they came, and filled both the ships, so that they began to sink.
8 When Simon Peter saw it, he fell down at Jesus' knees, saying, Depart from me; for I am a sinful man, O Lord.
9 For he was astonished, and all that were with him, at the draught of the fishes which they had taken:
10 And so was also James, and John, the sons of Zebedee, which were partners with Simon. And Jesus said unto Simon, Fear not; from henceforth thou shalt catch men.
11 And when they had brought their ships to land, they forsook all, and followed him.

One of the most powerful examples of giving and receiving because of partial obedience in the Bible, is the story in Luke 5:1-11 which details the day when Jesus commandeered Peter's boat in order to further his mission of preaching the Gospel.

THE SOVEREIGNTY OF GOD

The first thing that we see with regard to how God chooses to bless us has to do with the SOVEREIGNTY of God. Verses 2 and 3a says, **2** *And saw two ships standing by the lake: but the fishermen were gone out of them, and were washing their nets.* **3** *And he entered into one of the ships, which was Simon's, and prayed him that he would thrust out a little from the land."*

Although there were two ships, Jesus chose the ship that belonged to Simon Peter. What causes God to choose to use or to bless some people over others, is an interesting and often puzzling conundrum. He does not choose us because of our moral perfection nor because of our perfect obedience. If those were the criteria for being chosen, both Peter and most of us, would have been excluded. Peter's boat was not chosen merely because it was available. In fact, both boats seem to have been similarly situated in proximity and equally available to Jesus. Simon Peter's boat was simply Jesus' choice. There is no rhyme, reason or theological explanation for why God chooses what and who He chooses. Although we can pontificate at length why God favored Abel's offering over Cain's, why He chose Noah to build the ark, why He called Abraham, why He loved Jacob but rejected Esau, or why He anointed David, redeemed Rahab, called Peter—or even appointed Judas, at the end of the day—after we have factored in all the faults and failure of the men and women of the Old and New Testament, at its lowest common denominator, the answer is still THE SOVEREIGNTY OF GOD (Exodus 33:19 and Romans 9:15).

THE NECESSITY OF FAILURE

The next thing we see that the two boats and their occupants had in common, is that they both had experienced FAILURE. Verse 2 says, *"they were washing their nets"* and verse 5 says, *"they had toiled all night and taken (caught) nothing."* In spite of their vast fishing experience and expertise, that night they experienced failure. It seems as if sometimes God uses our failures as opportunities to test our faith. In this case, Jesus enters into the boat that belongs to Simon Peter, interrupts his plans for early retirement (at least for the night) and challenges him to *"launch out a little from the land."* (v. 3) Essentially He says to Peter, 'Try again what failed before. But this time do it for me.' Without a leasing contract, partnership agreement, an insurance rider or a promise of remittance, Jesus becomes Peter's newest business partner. May I suggest to any Minister, or even entrepreneur, who may be reading this book that possibly the real secret to your success is to stop working for yourself and to start "working for Jesus." If your product becomes a Ministry, you will always have a Market! Your "product" doesn't have to be preaching but it should be ministry. For the first time in Peter's life, his boat becomes a pulpit and he becomes vicariously, and maybe even unwittingly involved in the Ministry of Jesus Christ. Verse 3b says, *"And he (Jesus) sat down and taught the people out of the ship."*

A PERSONAL CHALLENGE

Verse 4 says, *"Now when He had left speaking, He said unto Simon, 'Launch out into the deep, let down your nets for a draught.'"* The word, draught, means *"a catching"* (Greek). In other words, Jesus is literally saying, what didn't work before will work now. Whether it is a matter of timing or whether it is a matter of location or whether it is simply the presence of Jesus or Peter's previous obedience, it is clear by Jesus' current challenge that something has changed.

THE INNER CONTENTION

The behavior of Simon Peter in verse 5 is a striking contrast to his behavior before. When Jesus entered the boat, Peter gave him no opposition. When Jesus commanded that he launch out a little from the land, Peter offered no challenge or resistance. But now that Jesus requires both SACRIFICE and SUSPENSION OF REASON, Peter offers a rebuttal. Peter says, *"Master, we have toiled all night and have taken nothing."* In other words, he says my **experience of failure is now hindering my faith.** Peter is looking back rather than looking forward and he is driven by emotion and intellect rather than by faith. Most of us, at some point or another, have experienced this tension between the failures of our past and the call to action to walk in renewed faith, when it looks like nothing has changed. It had never flooded before when God told Noah to build an ark. There was no lamb present when Abraham said to Isaac that God would "provide himself a lamb" on top of Mt. Moriah. And the widow at Zarephath of Zidon was still in a famine when Elijah said to her, *"bring me a little water in a cup"* and *"make for me a little cake first."*

The scriptures are replete with challenges of faith that of necessity, are met with inner contention because circumstances haven't changed. Even in our own personal lives, how many times has God challenged you to give or to do what seemed inconvenient and incongruous with your current circumstances? The simple truth is that FAITH DOESN'T MAKE SENSE!

PETER'S COMPROMISE OF INCOMPLETE OBEDIENCE

Any parent who has ever dealt with an impetuous teenager who thought that you wouldn't notice their intentional, yet seeming respectful disobedience, disguised as obedience should immediately recognize Peter's attempt at disobedience without appearing to disregard the Word of God or to disrespect the person and presence of Jesus. In response to Jesus' command to *"let down the nets..."* in verse 4, Peter answered in verse 5b, *"nevertheless at thy word I will let down the net."* Here Peter feigns obedience in the most religious and respectful way imaginable, by saying *"nevertheless, at thy word..."*. He obviously assumed either that Jesus wouldn't notice or that it wouldn't matter. But what Peter failed to realize is that PARTIAL OBEDIENCE IS STILL DISOBEDIENCE. Furthermore, Peter underestimated the AMOUNT OF THE HARVEST because he didn't comprehend THE WEIGHT OF THE PROMISE. Whatever God intends with "nets" can't be contained in one "net." Whenever God asks for "nets" and we only give him a "net," the result is that we are unable to handle the overflow and we end up broke because we didn't anticipate our season of more than enough. Verse 6 says, *"And when they had this done, they enclosed a multitude of fishes: and their net brake."*

THE IMPORTANCE OF PARTNERSHIP

In every human and divine endeavor, partnerships are necessary and essential. Verse 7 says, *"And they beckoned unto their partners, which were in the other ship, that they should come and help them. And they came, and filled both the ships, so that they began to sink."* In other words, Peter was trying to fill one net with what was intended for two ships! When God chose Peter's ship, He already knew that the provision would be enough for both ships. When we consider the narrative of Peter and "the miraculous draught of fishes," it is important to realize that whenever God asks for a SEED of sacrifice and obedience, He has a particular HARVEST in mind. Anything less than what He asks for will not be sufficient to contain the intended harvest of blessing and overflow. God gives us partners not just for where we are but also for where we're going. One of my favorite Old Testament references that is germane to this point is chronicled in Numbers 13:23, which says that when the children of Israel came into the land of promise, one branch of a cluster of grapes was so big that it took two men to carry it!

> **23** And they came unto the brook of Eshcol, and cut down from thence a branch with one cluster of grapes, and they bare it between two upon a staff; and they brought of the pomegranates, and of the figs.

Sometimes God gives us partners (whether in ministry or in life) who are patient enough to walk (and even toil) with us during our seasons of failure so that when our season of reaping comes, they can help us not only carry the harvest but also enjoy the fruit of it. Like Peter's partners in the other boat, sometimes we need to consider that just because we don't need certain people now, doesn't mean that they won't be necessary to keep us from sinking later.

Ecclesiastes 4:9-12 says, *"Two are better than one; because they have a good reward for their labour.*

For if they fall, the one will lift up his fellow; but woe to him that is alone when he falleth, for he hath not another to help him up...and a threefold cord is not easily broken."

A threefold cord represents partnership of soul, body and spirit.

Something To Offer

OUTLINE # 10

Seedtime And Harvest

ENESIS 8:20-22

> 20 *And Noah built an altar unto the Lord; and took of every clean beast, and of every clean fowl, and offered burnt offerings on the altar.*
> 21 *And the Lord smelled a sweet savour; and the Lord said in his heart, I will not again curse the ground any more for man's sake; for the imagination of man's heart is evil from his youth; neither will I again smite any more every thing living, as I have done.*
> 22 *While the earth remaineth, seedtime and harvest, and cold and heat, and summer and winter, and day and night shall not cease.*

This text comes at the conclusion of the flood in Genesis chapters 6-8 which brought judgment upon the wickedness that was in the earth. Chapter 6:8 says, *"But Noah found grace in the eyes of the Lord."* There are several types and shadows that exist in the story of the flood.

SOMETHING TO OFFER

Prior to the flood Enoch, which means "dedicated" (Hebrew), walked with God and was translated into Heaven (Genesis 5:24) as a type of the rapture. During the flood Noah, which means "rest" (Hebrew), walked with God (Genesis 6:9) as a type of Israel preserved during the Tribulation. The Ark becomes a type of refuge from judgment for believers. Grace in the midst of judgment becomes the basis for the rest of Noah's life. God gives him to build an Ark. God gives him instructions which include the materials, the architectural design and the nautical specifications for the ark including its' length, breadth and height. It is important to note that the ark has 3 stories (a type of the 1st, 2nd and 3rd Heaven) 1 door (a type of Christ) and 1 window (a type of future outpouring of the Holy Spirit when the dove is released in chapter 8:11.

In chapter 6:14, God tells Noah to *"pitch it within and without with pitch."* The word pitch, *"kopher"* (Hebrew) is the same word that is translated as "redemption, ransom or atonement." In other words, the ark is covered within and without by the redemption and atonement by Jesus Christ. It becomes a representation or type of the believer's "position" in Christ being "saved by Grace." Noah preached 120 years before the flood, it rained 40 days and 40 nights, and the rain was at its peak upon the face of the earth for 150 days or 5 months (which is a type of Grace). The ark rested upon Mt. Ararat, which means "the curse is reversed" (Hebrew), in the 7th month (a type of perfection and completion). In the 10th month the tops of the mountains were seen. God allowed Noah to exit the ark after a year and two months during which time God gave him grace to save his family and two of every living creature, both male and female.

. . .

This event initiates the Third dispensation. The First Dispensation was The Dispensation of Innocence which was initiated with "Edenic Covenant" and continued from the creation of Adam and Eve until their expulsion from the Garden of Eden.

The Second Dispensation was the Dispensation of Conscience which began with the expulsion of Adam and Eve and continued until the flood. The Third Dispensation is the Dispensation of Human Government. It begins with the flood and continues until the Tower of Babel. It also initiates the Noahic Covenant which was confirmed with the sign of the rainbow.

The ark represents salvation and the alter represents sacrifice. In response to the Grace of God over Noah's life he BUILDS AN ALTAR unto the Lord:

A. Noah offered burnt offerings unto the Lord of every clean beast and of every clean fowl which represented sanctification.
B. The Lord smelled a "Sweet Savour" which represented **worship**; Sweet (*"Nichowach"*) (Hebrew) Pleasant, soothing, delight; Savour (*"Reyach"*) (Hebrew) Odor, fragrance, aroma, odor of soothing
C. Three-fold Promise:

1. I will not curse the ground again for man's sake.
2. I will not smite everything living again. Smite means to beat, slay, kill, destroy.
3. I will restore continually with reciprocity from the earth for EVERY seed sown.

SEEDTIME AND HARVEST

The only thing between the seed and the harvest is time. There are primarily 4 words for time in scripture:

• **Chronos** (Greek) represents **chronological time**; time in order; determined by the clock

• **Kairos** (Greek) represents **prophetic time**; the set time (determined in heaven)

• **Moedim** (Hebrew) is **appointed times**; typically, times of commemoration and celebration to remind us in the present of God's faithfulness in the past in order to carry us into the future; where past, present and future come into alignment (determined by the calendar as in the 7 jewish feasts)

• **Hora** (Greek) means **hour**; the time for a preordained purpose; (John 2:4)

The importance of seedtime and harvest is that the harvest is built into the DNA of the seed. It is not based upon external circumstances nor is it controlled by the economy or by political exigencies. The law of seedtime and harvest is controlled by god alone.

Galatians 6:7-9

> *⁷ Do not be deceived, God is not mocked; for whatever a man sows, that he will also reap. ⁸ For he who sows to his flesh will of the flesh reap corruption, but he who sows to the Spirit will of the Spirit reap everlasting life. ⁹ And let us not grow weary while doing good, for in due season we shall reap if we do not lose heart.*

Something To Offer

OUTLINE # 11

No Man Can Serve Two Masters

Matthew 6:24-33

24 No man can serve two masters: for either he will hate the one, and love the other; or else he will hold to the one, and despise the other. Ye cannot serve God and mammon.

25 Therefore I say unto you, Take no thought for your life, what ye shall eat, or what ye shall drink; nor yet for your body, what ye shall put on. Is not the life more than meat, and the body than raiment?

26 Behold the fowls of the air: for they sow not, neither do they reap, nor gather into barns; yet your heavenly Father feedeth them. Are ye not much better than they?

27 Which of you by taking thought can add one cubit unto his stature?

28 And why take ye thought for raiment? Consider the lilies of the field, how they grow; they toil not, neither do they spin:

29 And yet I say unto you, That even Solomon in all his glory was not arrayed like one of these.

30 Wherefore, if God so clothe the grass of the field, which to day is, and to morrow is cast into the oven, shall he not much more clothe you, O ye of little faith?

31 Therefore take no thought, saying, What shall we eat? or, What shall we drink? or, Wherewithal shall we be clothed?

32 (For after all these things do the Gentiles seek:) for your heavenly Father knoweth that ye have need of all these things.

33 But seek ye first the kingdom of God, and his righteousness; and all these things shall be added unto you.

In our current discussion I want to focus primarily on verse 24 of Matthew 6 in the context of the teachings of Jesus with regard to money. For the purposes of this discourse let us begin by looking at the superscription for verses 19-24.

THE KINGDOM LAW OF RICHES

The concept of wealth not being a substitute for faith is not new. In Proverbs 10:15, Solomon writes, *"The rich man's wealth is his strong city..."* and in Proverbs 18:11 he continues the same thought, *"The rich man's wealth is his strong city, and as a high wall in his own conceit."*

The idea is not that wealth is bad but that trusting in wealth (riches and material things) leads to a false confidence in things that pertain to this world and a false hope with regard to eternity. Even in the teachings of Jesus verses, like Matthew 19:23-24 (repeated in each of the synoptic gospels in Mark 10:24-25 and Luke 18:24-25) are often misinterpreted and misunderstood.

Matthew 19:23-24

> ***23*** *Then said Jesus unto his disciples, Verily I say unto you, That a rich man shall hardly enter into the kingdom of heaven.*
> ***24*** *And again I say unto you, It is easier for a camel to go through the eye of a needle, than for a rich man to enter into the kingdom of God.*

These texts are often mistaken as teachings against the acquisition of material wealth. Upon careful reflection and contextual examination, however, we see that Jesus is not teaching against wealth or riches, but he is rather, teaching against trust or confidence in riches as a means of access into the Kingdom of Heaven. When he says that it is *"easier for a camel to go through the eye of a needle, than for rich man to enter into the Kingdom of God,"* whether he is using hyperbole (as some scholars suspect) or, whether this is an historic reference to a small gate in Jerusalem known as "The Needle's Eye," (as some writers as early as the 13th and 15th centuries suggested), what is without question is that Jesus is saying that in order for those who have riches and great wealth to enter into the Kingdom of Heaven, the weight of their possessions can never be more of a priority than the weight of Christian responsibility, faith, sacrifice and obedience. As was the case with the "rich young ruler" the value of temporal possessions must never outweigh the value of eternal life. Jesus is not merely talking about material possessions; he is talking about the **motive for** and the **manner** in which we acquire and use wealth in advancement of the Kingdom. The issue focuses more on PRIORITIES than on POSSESSIONS.

. . .

SOMETHING TO OFFER

In Matthew 6:19-21 Jesus warns us that earthly possessions are temporary and that what we hold as dear in our hands is a reflection of what we value in our hearts.

In verse 24, Jesus addresses the need for determining **allegiance** and **obedience** with regard to the juxtaposition of God and money.

> No man can serve two masters: for either
> he will hate the one, and love the other;
> or else he will hold to the one, and
> despise the other. Ye cannot serve God
> and mammon. Matthew 6:24

The term serve, *"douleuo"* (Greek), means "to be a slave to or to be in bondage, whether literally or figuratively, voluntarily or involuntarily; to obey." A master, *"kyrios"* (Greek) is one who exercises "supreme authority or control; possessor or disposer of a person or thing." Of course, the idea of serving two masters becomes more critical whenever their goals, plans, purposes or desires conflict. In such cases, Jesus reminds us that our choices determine priority and that obedience determines allegiance. *"Either he will hate the one and love the other; or else he will hold the one and despise the other. Ye cannot serve God and mammon."* The word mammon, *"mammonas"* (Greek) means "wealth, riches, money." The tension between God and money occurs primarily when two things happen: when faith requires what fear opposes or refuses to release, or when faith requires what greed denies and holds onto.

. . .

The two greatest enemies of Faith with regard to money are **fear** and **greed**. In both cases the issue becomes who will you obey and to whom is your allegiance? Is your covenant with God or with mammon?

In Hebrews 11:6 we are admonished that, *"Without faith it is impossible to please God, he that cometh to Him must believe that He is; and that He is a rewarder of them that diligently seek him."*

Romans 14:23 says, *"... whatever is not of faith is sin."*

THE LAW OF FAITH

Matthew 6:25-31 addresses the idea of freedom from anxiety and worry while trusting confidently in God's care. In this section of scripture, Jesus outlines the PROCESS by which we PRACTICE faith:

1. *"Take no thought for your life"*

The mere thought of this concept requires EMOTIONAL DIVESTITURE.

In 1 Peter 5:7, Peter describes it as *"casting all your cares upon him for he careth for you."* The phrase "take no thought" is interesting because in the Greek it is the phrase *"me' merimnao"* which means "not to be anxious, not to look out for, or to promote one's interests; not to be overwhelmed with responsibility for care or concern." Here, he specifically talks about food, drink and clothes. Of course he does not literally mean, don't think about these things. What he is saying is that, as believers, we should never be overcome with fear nor overwhelmed with worry about things that are not within our control. He is not saying to be irresponsible, but he is saying that we must always remember that we are HIS responsibility. Just as children are the responsibility of their parents and citizens are the responsibility of those who govern, as Children of God and citizens of the Kingdom of God, we are His responsibility. God says that if He takes care of the birds of the air and the lilies of the field, as His children we should be confident in his care for us. Simply put, worry and anxiety are the result of a LACK OF FAITH. In Matthew 6:30, he says, " *Wherefore, if God so clothe the grass of the field, which today is and tomorrow is cast into the oven, shall he not much more clothe you, O ye of little faith?*"

In Philippians 4:6, Paul writes, *"Be careful for nothing; but in every thing by prayer and supplication with thanksgiving let your requests be made known unto God."*

In Matthew 6:32 Jesus reminds us, that *"your Heavenly Father knoweth that ye have need of all these things."* I remember years ago going to a certain restaurant in our area. Because I was hungry, I ordered a burger. Within a matter of minutes after getting my food I suddenly got full. I sat outside on the patio hoping that my appetite would come back, and I heard the Holy Spirit say, "leave it on the table." Although I felt guilty for wasting money and food, I reluctantly obeyed. As I walked away, I looked back and saw several birds eating what I had paid for. I then realized that God was showing me how he uses us to care for others and uses others to care for us!

2. *"But seek ye first the kingdom of God, and his righteousness; and all these things shall be added unto you."* The word seek, "Zeteo" (Greek) means "to seek in order to find, to desire, to enquire, to search, to crave, strive after; by extension, to worship."

KINGDOM PRIORITIES

"But seek ye first the Kingdom of God" requires that the priorities of the Kingdom must be our priorities.

Romans 14:17 admonishes that "The Kingdom of God is not meat and drink; but, righteousness, peace and joy in the Holy Ghost."

Kingdom priorities, then, are not physical nor material; they are not "meat and drink."

They are threefold:

1. Righteousness - "Dikaiosyne" (Greek) that is, "justice, virtue, integrity, purity of heart and mind" by extension, righteous acts and a moral witness
2. Peace - "eirene" (Greek) which is "tranquillity, harmony, security, felicity"; inner peace
3. Joy - "chara" (Greek) which is "cheerfulness, calm delight, gladness."

KINGDOM PASSION

The righteousness of God is expressed through presence and power.

KINGDOM PROVISION

"Shall be added" is the Greek word, *"prostithemi,"* which means "to lay beside, to increase, annex, add to"

The idea here, is that when you "seek" the Kingdom, you don't have to seek provisions. We don't have to seek for tires when you get a car. You don't have to seek for windows or a roof when you get a house. When you get the Kingdom, it comes with PROVISIONS.

A FRESH LOOK AT THE PARABLE OF THE TALENTS: WHAT HAPPENS WHEN MONEY BECOMES THE MASTER?

Matthew 25:14-30

14 For the kingdom of heaven is as a man traveling into a far country, who called his own servants, and delivered unto them his goods.

15 And unto one he gave five talents, to another two, and to another one; to every man according to his several ability; and straightway took his journey.

16 Then he that had received the five talents went and traded with the same, and made them other five talents.

17 And likewise he that had received two, he also gained other two.

18 But he that had received one went and digged in the earth, and hid his lord's money.

19 After a long time the lord of those servants cometh, and reckoneth with them.

20 And so he that had received five talents came and brought other five talents, saying, Lord, thou deliveredst unto me five talents: behold, I have gained beside them five talents more.

21 His lord said unto him, Well done, thou good and faithful servant: thou hast been faithful over a few things, I will make thee ruler over many things: enter thou into the joy of thy lord.

22 He also that had received two talents came and said, Lord, thou deliveredst unto me two talents: behold, I have gained two other talents beside them.

23 His lord said unto him, Well done, good and faithful servant; thou hast been faithful over a few things, I will make thee ruler over many things: enter thou into the joy of thy lord.

24 Then he which had received the one talent came and said, Lord, I knew thee that thou art an hard man, reaping where thou hast not sown, and gathering where thou hast not strawed:

25 And I was afraid, and went and hid thy talent in the earth: lo, there thouahast that is thine.

26 His lord answered and said unto him, Thou wicked and slothful servant, thou knewest that I reap where I sowed not, and gather where I have not strawed:

²⁷ Thou oughtest therefore to have put my money to the exchangers, and then at my coming I should have received mine own with usury.

²⁸ Take therefore the talent from him, and give it unto him which hath ten talents.

²⁹ For unto every one that hath shall be given, and he shall have abundance: but from him that hath not shall be taken away even that which he hath.

³⁰ And cast ye the unprofitable servant into outer darkness: there shall be weeping and gnashing of teeth.

The traditional interpretation and brief synopsis of "The Parable of the Talents" is that of a man who while traveling to a far country calls three of his servants and delivers unto them his goods *"hyparchonta"* (Greek)"property, possessions, wealth". He gives 5 talents *"talanton,"* (Greek) "a sum of money" to one servant, 2 talents to another servant and 1 talent to the last servant *"according to their several ability."* (v. 16) It should be noted that in Israel, a talent of silver weighed about 100 pounds and a talent of gold weighed about 200 pounds. In the absence of their "lord," the servant who had the 5 talents traded *"ergazomai"* (Greek) "to work, labor; occupation; to do business" and produced five other talents. Similarly, the servant who had 2 talents produced two more. The servant who only had 1 talent *"went and digged in the earth and buried his lord's money"* (v.18) After a long time away, their lord returned to reckon with his servants. Being pleased with the profitability of the two servants who gained increase on his investment, he said unto them, *"Well done thy good and faithful servant(s), thou hast been faithful over few things, I will make thee ruler over many things: enter thou into the joy of thy lord."* (vv. 22,23)

When he encountered the servant who had 1 talent, he was displeased that he had buried it and returned it without profit saying, *"Thou wicked and slothful servant, thou knewest that I reap where I sowed not, and gather where I have not strawed:*

Thou oughtest therefore to have put my money to the exchangers, and then at my coming I would have received mine own with usury." (vv.26-27) Their lord then took the one talent from him and gave it unto the one who had 10 talents. He then said, *"For unto every one that hath shall be given and he shall have abundance: but from him that hath not shall be taken away even that which he hath."* (v.29) And he casted the *"unprofitable servant into outer darkness..."* Typically, this parable is taught to describe what the Kingdom of Heaven is like. But, what if, especially in the context of the 2nd part of the discourse with regard to the test of Gentile nations (vv. 31-46), the Parable of the Talents is a description of what the Kingdom of Heaven "is not." A careful reading of the parable seems to describe the "Kingdom" from a western, capitalistic perspective where the only thing that matters is PROFIT and PROFITABILITY.

- .The lord distributes money and expects profit through trading;
- 2. The lord endorses usury (which is condemned throughout scripture, including Exodus 22:25, Deuteronomy 23:19 and Psalm 15:5); and,
- 3. The lord takes from those that "have not" in order to give to those that "have."

THE HAVES AND THE HAVE NOTS

When money is MASTER and PROFIT becomes the only motivation and criteria for reward, then the "HAVE NOTS" suffer at the hands and for the benefit of the "HAVES." It seems to me that our traditional, western capitalistic interpretation of the parable makes "GOD A CAPITALIST" and makes their version of the "KINGDOM OF HEAVEN" a system where the rich get richer and the poor are cast into "outer darkness." If we consider this "outer darkness" not from a spiritual or eschatological construct, but rather as a social phenomenon where we embrace a system fueled by fear and where those who "have not" are cast into the "outer darkness" into abyss of homelessness, hunger, poverty and prison, then Jesus' criticism and condemnation of the Gentile nations for their lack of compassion and care for the "least of these" (v.40) would make sense.

Matthew 25:31-46

> *31 When the Son of man shall come in his glory, and all the holy angels with him, then shall he sit upon the throne of his glory:*
> *32 And before him shall be gathered all nations: and he shall separate them one from another, as a shepherd divideth his sheep from the goats:*
> *33 And he shall set the sheep on his right hand, but the goats on the left.*
> *34 Then shall the King say unto them on his right hand, Come, ye blessed of my Father, inherit the kingdom prepared for you from the foundation of the world:*
> *35 For I was an hungred, and ye gave me meat: I was thirsty, and ye gave me drink: I was a stranger, and ye took me in:*
> *36 Naked, and ye clothed me: I was sick, and ye visited me: I was in prison, and ye came unto me.*
> *37 Then shall the righteous answer him, saying, Lord, when saw we thee an hungred, and fed thee? or thirsty, and gave thee drink?*
> *38 When saw we thee a stranger, and took thee in? or naked, and clothed thee?*

39 Or when saw we thee sick, or in prison, and came unto thee?

40 And the King shall answer and say unto them, Verily I say unto you, Inasmuch as ye have done it unto one of the least of these my brethren, ye have done it unto me.

41 Then shall he say also unto them on the left hand, Depart from me, ye cursed, into everlasting fire, prepared for the devil and his angels:

42 For I was an hungred, and ye gave me no meat: I was thirsty, and ye gave me no drink:

43 I was a stranger, and ye took me not in: naked, and ye clothed me not: sick, and in prison, and ye visited me not.

44 Then shall they also answer him, saying, Lord, when saw we thee an hungred, or athirst, or a stranger, or naked, or sick, or in prison, and did not minister unto thee?

45 Then shall he answer them, saying, Verily I say unto you, Inasmuch as ye did it not to one of the least of these, ye did it not to me.

46 And these shall go away into everlasting punishment: but the righteous into life eternal.

THE MORALITY OF MONEY

When money becomes the master, then the love of money becomes the motive and only the servants who are "profitable" get the reward. This interpretation makes "usury" a virtue and makes greed the reward. That's not the kingdom of Heaven: that's the kingdom of this world! Maybe Jesus is telling us that the Kingdom of Heaven is the place where money must not become the master, but where it must be mastered by a God who is moral, compassionate and concerned for *"the least of these."*

In the Kingdom of Heaven, money has a MISSION and a MANDATE that is not connected to PROFIT and GREED!

Something To Offer

OUTLINE # 12

Money In The Mouth Of The Fish

Matthew 17:24-27

> 24 And when they were come to Capernaum, they that received tribute money came to Peter, and said, Doth not your master pay tribute?
> 25 He saith, Yes. And when he was come into the house, Jesus prevented him, saying, What thinkest thou, Simon? of whom do the kings of the earth take custom or tribute? of their own children, or of strangers?
> 26 Peter saith unto him, Of strangers. Jesus saith unto him, Then are the children free.
> 27 Notwithstanding, lest we should offend them, go thou to the sea, and cast an hook, and take up the fish that first cometh up; and when thou hast opened his mouth, thou shalt find a piece of money: that take, and give unto them for me and thee.

Our primary text begins with a conversation between Peter

and the tax collectors. Peter is possibly making arrangements with those who collect the "tribute money" as the context of the scripture seems to imply that Peter's taxes are due and possibly even past due. While engaged in taking care of what appears to be his personal business, those who receive the taxes also enquire about Jesus and the payment of his taxes. Peter's response indicates his awareness of Jesus' tax obligation as well. When Peter returns to the house, Jesus begins to ask questions about the legitimacy of taxation. This line of communication indicates to Peter that Jesus has been privy to the previous conversation. In anticipation of Peter's concern in verse 25 Jesus says to Peter, *"What thinketh thou Simon? Of whom do the Kings of the earth take custom or tribute? Of their children or from strangers? Peter answered unto him, of strangers. Jesus said unto him, then are the children free."* This brief discourse confirms three things: firstly, that as a Prophet, Jesus is aware both of the complaint of the officials in order to defame him and of Peter's concern in order to defend him. And secondly, that the theological interpretation of both taxes and offerings deals with the issues of relationship and responsibility. This idea is clarified in Jesus' discussion with the Pharisees and the Herodians in Matthew 22:15-22, Mark 12:13-17 and Luke 20:19-26.

In these companion texts, the Pharisees and Herodians seek to "entangle" Jesus in an effort to bring accusations of treason against him. They ask, *"Is it lawful to give tribute unto Caesar, or not?"* In response to this question, knowing that they were trying to tempt him, Jesus asked them to bring him a coin and asked whose image and superscription was on the coin? When they answered, "Caesar's," Jesus then replied, *"Render therefore unto Caesar the things that are Caesar's and unto God the things that are God's."* Here Jesus reinforces the idea of governmental authority and argues that those who are under the authority of Caesar have the responsibility to pay Him tribute from what is His. By the same logic then, Jesus argues that since man was created in the image of God, we are to render unto God those things that are God's. Here Jesus reinforces the Old Testament doctrine from Genesis 1:27 that man was created in the image of God (*"imago dei"*), reestablishes his authority as the Son of God and alludes to his incarnation as "God in the flesh." The New Testament further reminds us in John 1:12 that *"as many as received him, to them gave he power to become the "sons of God"* and in Romans 8:29 that we have been predestined to be *"conformed to the image of his dear son."* What started out as a trap now, becomes a theological discourse on RELATIONSHIP and RESPONSIBILITY.

Thirdly, Jesus is concerned about offense. The word, "offend," "*skandalizo*" (Greek) means "to entrap, entice to sin; to put a stumbling block or impediment in the way; to cause distrust." He says in verse 27 that this MIRACLE OF PROVISION IS GIVEN IN ORDER TO PREVENT OFFENSE. It's important to remember that, as a believer God is concerned about our reputation. Remember in Genesis 12:2-3 God told Abram, "I will make your name great...". I in Ecclesiastes 7:1 Solomon says, "A good name is better than precious ointment...," and in Acts 1:8 one of the reasons that we are given the Holy Spirit is protect our witness.

Notwithstanding, lest we should offend them, go thou to the sea, and cast an hook, and take up the fish that first cometh up; and when thou hast opened his mouth, thou shalt find a piece of money: that take, and give unto them for me and thee. Matthew 7:27

1. He gives DETAILED INSTRUCTIONS; "Go thou to the sea, and cast a hook"

2. He promises IMMEDIATE RESPONSE; "Take up the fish that first cometh up"

3. He gives INTRUSION AND ACCESS; "When thou hast openeth his mouth"

4. He promises INTERRUPTED PROCESS the fish ate the money, but he couldn't swallow it. If he had swallowed it, he couldn't have digested it. In other words, when God is giving you a miracle of supernatural provision, He will give someone else the appetite for something that you need, allow them to go get it, and then not let them consume it, because even though it's in their mouth; it's still yours. In the fish put Jonah in his mouth, he swallowed him, but he couldn't consume him; because, even in his disobedience, Jonah still belonged to God! The wealth of the sinner is laid up for the righteous (Proverbs 13:22)

5. He provides INTERCESSION AND INTERVENTION BY INTERMEDIARIES on your behalf: *"Take and give unto them for me and for thee."*

-Jesus tells Peter that there will be enough money in the mouth of one fish to pay your taxes and mine!

EPILOGUE

Sacrificial Giving

There are basically 3 Types of Sacrificial Giving.

GIVING OUT OF LACK

Mark 12:41-44

> *41 And Jesus sat over against the treasury, and beheld how the people cast money into the treasury: and many that were rich cast in much.*
>
> *42 And there came a certain poor widow, and she threw in two mites, which make a farthing.*
>
> *43 And he called unto him his disciples, and saith unto them, Verily I say unto you, That this poor widow hath cast more in, than all they which have cast into the treasury:*
>
> *44 For all they did cast in of their abundance; but she of her want did cast in all that she had, even all her living.*

The story of the Widow's Mite has always intrigued me. The fact that Jesus watched as the people came to give is interesting but what is most interesting to me is that as he watched those who were rich give much into the temple treasury, HE WATCHED IN SILENCE. He was unmoved by their offerings because their offerings were not SACRIFICIAL. Many times when we give, we give out of comfort and convenience rather than out of sacrifice and covenant. As Jesus watched, the text says, *"And there came a certain poor widow, and she threw in two mites, which make a farthing. And he called into him his disciples and said unto them, Verily I say unto you that this poor widow hath cast more in, than all they that have cast into the treasury: for all they did cast in of their abundance; but she of her want did cast in all that she had, even all her living."* (vv.42-44) She got the attention of Jesus not because of how much she gave but because of how little she had left.

I remember in the early years of my pastorate as a young man in my early 20's there was an older Mother in our church who was on a fixed income. She was probably 70 or 80 years old. One day she came to me and said, "Pastor, I want you to pray with me." She explained that her light bill was due and that she wasn't sure how she was going to pay it. Of course, I asked her how much it was and told her that the Church or I could help her. I will never forget what she said to me that day. She said, as if she was almost insulted, "Pastor, I didn't ask for money. I asked for prayer. Prayer can do more than money." As a young Pastor, I was both embarrassed and impressed that when my first response was carnal, she had taught such a profound spiritual lesson of faith. Well, I didn't know it then, but the lessons that she would teach me over the next few weeks and months and years were just beginning. On her way out of my small office in that little church she said, "and while I'm here I need to pay my tithes." I immediately said, "No mother, let's wait until you can take care of the light bill and then you can pay your tithes." She just looked at me with amazement, confusion and consternation. As I prayed with her concerning her financial need, the Holy Spirit rebuked me for my biblical error regarding the tithe. When I finished praying I said, "Mother, let me take your tithes and bless them." She then smiled and said, "Pastor, I know your heart is right, but I knew you were wrong when you told me to keep my tithes. I just prayed for you because I know you love God, and you love us." She paused, and said, "I just said, 'Lord, help my little young Pastor because sometimes he doesn't know what he's doing.'" We both laughed. She said, "as long as I've been saved, I know that I can't steal God's tithe. I may have been a lot of things in my life, but I've never been a thief. I will starve before I steal." She just laughed, said "I love you, Pastor" and went out of the door.

Over the next several weeks whenever I would see her, I would ask if she had paid the light bill and she would always say, "No, but the lights are still on." I honestly think that I was more worried about it than she was. Every week she would give me the same response, "No, but the lights are still on." Then one Sunday about six months later, she came into the Church down the aisle, praising God. I assumed that God had given her a financial miracle. When I asked her about the light bill she said, "Pastor, you're not going to believe what happened!" She said, "a young man came to my door and told me that they sent him to check on me because they knew that I didn't have any lights. I invited him in and flipped the switch and when the lights came on, he turned pale as a ghost! I thought he was gonna faint!" She said, "he took me outside in the back of the house and showed me that they had taken my meter out!" She said the young man explained to her that her lights could not be on with no meter! She said that she took him inside and flipped the switch again and said to him what she had been saying for months, "Young man, I know what you are saying, but the lights are still on!" I think they put another meter in for Mother on some special program. And I'm not sure that she ever had to pay another light bill again! Like that widow in the Bible, HER FAITH AND SACRIFICE GOT THE ATTENTION OF JESUS!

The text says that because she gave out of her want, she had given more than everyone else. It was not the quantity of her offering, but the quality that impressed Jesus. Her offering of two small copper coins were worth about 1/8 of a cent in today's currency but it caused Jesus to use her as an example of SACRIFICIAL GIVING because she gave what she had and because of how little she had left.

GIVING OUT OF LOVE

In Matthew 26:7-13 (Mark 14:3-7; Luke 7:37-39 and John 12:2-8)

> *7 There came unto him a woman having an alabaster box of very precious ointment, and poured it on his head, as he sat at meat.*
> *8 But when his disciples saw it, they had indignation, saying, To what purpose is this waste?*
> *9 For this ointment might have been sold for much, and given to the poor.*
> *10 When Jesus understood it, he said unto them, Why trouble ye the woman? for she hath wrought a good work upon me.*
> *11 For ye have the poor always with you; but me ye have not always.*
> *12 For in that she hath poured this ointment on my body, she did it for my burial.*
> *13 Verily I say unto you, Wheresoever this gospel shall be preached in the whole world, there*

shall also this, that this woman hath done, be told for a memorial of her.

The story of the woman with the alabaster box who broke the box and poured out precious ointment of spikenard to anoint the head of Jesus is mentioned in all three of the synoptic gospels, and in the book of John (although the woman in Luke appears to be different and the place appears to be different.) Matthew, Mark and John identify the woman as Mary of Bethany while Luke does not identify the woman. Matthew and Mark say that the anointing took place in Bethany in the house of Simon the Leper, while John's gospel says that the anointing took place at a house in Bethany where Martha served. The woman in Luke anoints the feet of Jesus at a dinner in a house of one of the Pharisees. In Matthew, Mark and John the woman anoints the head of Jesus. It appears then, that there were at least three times when Jesus was anointed with costly perfumed oil by at least two women.

What is similar about the women and their offerings is that:

1. The gift was SUBSTANTIAL.

The narratives of both Mark and John mention that the oil that was used in Mary's offering could have been sold for 300 pence," which would have equaled about a year's wages. (v. 5)

2. The gift was SACRIFICIAL.

The fact that the oil had been stored in an alabaster box indicates that it was not only costly but that it had been saved for a special purpose The box had to be broken in order for the oil to be used.

3. The gift was SUITABLE.

In both Matthew and Mark, Jesus implied that the woman's

offering of sacrifice would be "preached for a Memorial of her." Jesus said that what she did was not wasteful extravagance; it was suitable. It was an offering of honor. It was substantial, it was sacrificial, but it was also suitable. It would be preached for a memorial. Because of her offering, she will never be forgotten; her name may not be on a building, but her name will be written as a memorial, on a monument, in Heaven and will be preached throughout the earth, throughout all ages

GIVING FOR THE SAKE OF ATONEMENT

2 Samuel 24:24-25

> **24** *And the king said unto Araunah, Nay; but I will surely buy it of thee at a price: neither will I offer burnt offerings unto the Lord my God of that which doth cost me nothing. So David bought the threshingfloor and the oxen for fifty shekels of silver.*
> **25** *And David built there an altar unto the Lord, and offered burnt offerings and peace offerings. So the Lord was intreated for the land, and the plague was stayed from Israel.*

In 2 Samuel Chapter 24, verses 24-25 judgment had come upon Israel because David had numbered the people of Israel and Judah (the Northern and Southern Kingdoms). In verses 10-14, David's heart was convicted, and he prayed that God would forgive him and take away his iniquity. In response to David's prayer God spoke to the Prophet Gad, David's seer, and gave him three options for punishment: seven years of famine in the land, fleeing three months from his enemies while they were in pursuit, or three days pestilence in the land.

In verse 14, David chose to "fall ... into the hands of Lord ...

rather than into the hands of man." *And David said unto Gad, I am in a great strait: let us fall now into the hand of the Lord; for his mercies are great: and let me not fall into the hand of man.*

And, in verse 15-16 God sent a pestilence upon the people and seventy thousand men died between Dan and Beersheba. Then the Lord sent an Angel to stay the hand of judgment from smiting the people. As the Angel stood by the threshing place of Araunah the Jebusite, David prayed again for mercy for the people in verse 17.

> **17** *And David spake unto the Lord when he saw the angel that smote the people, and said, Lo, I have sinned, and I have done wickedly: but these sheep, what have they done? let thine hand, I pray thee, be against me, and against my father's house.*

In verse 18, the Prophet Gad returned to David for him to *"Go up, rear an altar unto the Lord in the threshingfloor of Araunah the Jebusite."*

In verses 20-21 David offers to buy the land in order to build the Altar "that the plague may be stayed from the people." And, in verses 22-23 Araunah offers to give David that is needed for the offering!

> **22** And Araunah said unto David, Let my lord the king take and offer up what seemeth good unto him: behold, here be oxen for burnt sacrifice, and threshing instruments and other instruments of the oxen for wood.
> **23** All these things did Araunah, as a king, give unto the king. And Araunah said unto the king, The Lord thy God accept thee.

In verses 24-25, David refuses to accept the gift on the grounds that he cannot offer a sacrifice that is not a sacrifice! As a matter of integrity, David buys what is offered as a gift. He buys both the threshingfloor and the oxen for the sacrifice for a price of fifty shekels of silver. It should also be noted that in 1 Chronicles 21:25 we are told that David purchased the land at the "full price" of six hundred shekels of gold. The reason for the difference in amounts is that the "threshingfloor" was a small area where grain was separated while the "threshing place" was the entire parcel of land. Historians calculate that fifty shekels of silver would be valued between $30 and $4800 due to fluctuating markets and that six hundred shekels of gold would have been valued between $4800 and $600,000! The point of course, is that either way, David paid dearly for what he couldn't have gotten for free. But as a gift it would not have been a SACRIFICE.

In 2 Samuel 24:25 and in 1 Chronicles 21:26-28, David built an altar and offered burnt offerings and peace offerings. And the plague stopped.

The Biblical construct of SACRIFICIAL GIVING revolves around one central concept: IT MUST BE A SACRIFICE! Whether it is given from little so that what remains is little, whether it is given from what has been set aside for another intended purpose or whether it is at a great personal and financial cost, a sacrifice must be in fact, a sacrifice. It must include inconvenience and intent.

Very often in the contemporary context of what we call sacrificial offerings, they are no more than another offering to help meet the budget. Also in a very real sense, they are rarely a genuine sacrifice unto the Lord.

I can think of several times when I felt impressed of the Holy Spirit to give a genuine sacrifice unto the Lord. Once we were raising money for renovations at our local church and on a Sunday morning, I felt the leading of the Lord to give a certain amount out of our savings. After consulting with my wife and considering the matter in prayer, we quickly released the seed. It opened the flood gates of giving for the project and we completed the renovations debt free!

Another time when my wife was pregnant with our first child, she was up watching Christian television late at night and a certain minister asked for a large seed. Although we were saving for the down payment for our first house, we both felt impressed of the Holy Spirit to release the seed. Within two weeks God miraculously put us in the position to purchase a house that we didn't even know was on the market.

Another time I was at a Conference and after a powerful move of God, the minister asked for a large seed and when I released it, God began to give specific prophetic direction and insight that blessed our lives and ministry for years! I could relate so many times when sacrificial giving has led to experiencing the miraculous but, to be honest and transparent, there have also been times when I have given sacrificially and seemingly nothing happened. Those are what I call "storehouse moments" where God takes the seed and stores it up for a "future need." Simply put, when God requires a SACRIFICE, it is never comfortable nor convenient and sometimes we are not even conscious or cognizant of what God is doing in that moment. Sacrificial giving is activated by the Holy Spirit through the gift of faith and in a moment of obedience, God supernaturally transports the seed into the soil of our lives in order to produce the intended harvest! When we give sacrificially, God gives us opportunity to give in three ways. Sometimes we give of our TREASURES, Sometimes we give of our TALENTS. Sometimes we give of our TIME, but there is never a moment when we are without an offering or without an opportunity! When we give, we do not give grudgingly nor of necessity. We give understanding that giving is an OPPORTUNITY and not merely an OBLIGATION. 2 Corinthians 9:7.

> *Every man according as he purposeth in his heart, so let him give; not grudgingly, or of necessity: for God loveth a cheerful giver.*

Whether much or little, remember that whenever God requires or desires an offering, we always have SOMETHING TO OFFER.

www.ingramcontent.com/pod-product-compliance
Lightning Source LLC
Chambersburg PA
CBHW062118080426
42734CB00012B/2902